TSUNAMI OF THE MIND

———◆———

STORIES OF TRAUMA, RECOVERY, AND HOPE

To Trez –
with thanks for your
love and care for all
our friends –
Barbara
6/15/17

Barbara Bate, PhD

ISBN: 1533468788
ISBN: 9781533468789
Library of Congress Control Number: 2016908682
CreateSpace Independent Publishing Platform
North Charleston, South Carolina
"The Mystery of Depression," from Parker Palmer, *Let Your Life Speak,* Copyright
Jossey Bass, 2000. Reprinted by permission of John Wiley & Sons, Inc.

THE MYSTERY OF DEPRESSION

Twice in my forties I spent endless months in the snake pit of the soul. Hour by hour, day by day, I wrestled with the desire to die, sometimes so feeble in my resistance that I "practiced" ways of doing myself in. I could feel nothing except the burden of my own life and the exhaustion, the apparent futility, of trying to sustain it.

I understand why some depressed people kill themselves: they need the rest. But I do not understand why others are able to find new life in the midst of a living death, though I am one of them. I can tell you what I did to survive and, eventually, to thrive—but I cannot tell you why I was able to do those things before it was too late.

Parker J. Palmer, Let Your Life Speak[1]

CONTENTS

ABOUT THIS BOOK

Tsunami of the Mind: *Stories of Trauma, Recovery, and Hope* is both personal and educational. The heart of the book is a series of conversations I've had with people who, like me, have lived through trauma, come close to suicide, and lived into recovery. All of them are survivors who chose to share their story with me and to allow it to be published.

The increase in suicides among women and the continuing high suicide rates among youth and older adult men are the subject of widespread speculation, but little understanding. Discussions about suicide continue to be largely taboo, and bipolar illness is sensationalized in the media without being recognized as having important variations.

This book uniquely addresses both suicide and bipolar illnesses. I myself am a survivor. Ten different men and women share their stories of trauma, suicide attempts, and survival. In nearly every instance, they experienced wrong diagnoses of their brain disorders, endangering their lives. Their recoveries are testament to their resilience.

These ten dialogues reveal a serious lack of knowledge about bipolar depression by health professionals, many of whom have used dangerously wrong medications to treat the problem. These conversations also confirm that the stigma about being treated for a "mental illness," i.e. a brain disorder, fosters shame and silence among the general public, and especially those who need and deserve that help.

Title. "Tsunami of the mind" is not a technical term, but a phrase created to illustrate a serious and sometimes fatal human phenomenon. These internal killer waves affect a great many people, including many living along the Pacific Northwest coast where I live. I know active, bright, and creative people who experience major changes in their energy level, sleep, eating, and moods that can switch from joy to despair. For reasons that are partly genetic and partly environmental, we can deplete our energy in intense activity and racing thoughts, and then become ashamed and disgusted with our sudden inability to do what we had done easily before. These unpredictable changes are confusing to the people experiencing them, and to the people who care about them. After a tsunami of the mind, many people find parts of their lives are damaged or destroyed.

Tsunami of the Mind tells about the lives of ten human beings. They became my friends through our conversations. I am not a clinician, but a peer. I coined the acronym PEER years ago, meaning a Person of Experience, Engaged in Recovery. The information these friends and I share in these conversations came from our experiences, and from my own decade of personal research into brain science, health, and recovery.

NOTE TO THE READER: More than half of the women and men you will meet in this book have experienced violence, including sexual abuse. Trauma affected their brains, and it impacted their struggles to stay alive. Their accounts are included in summary form in the interviews. I recognize that reading about traumatic events can trigger strong emotions, and it may not be appropriate for all readers. Please make sure that you are in contact with someone you trust as you read about these individuals' difficult experiences.

Names of medicines used by people in this book are included when mentioned specifically by that person. As the stories indicate, no medicine works the same way for every individual, and medicines can have both positive and negative effects. I encourage readers to educate themselves about medications, foods, and supplements. Please discuss that information thoroughly with others, including but not limited to health professionals.

This book is not an attack on primary care physicians, therapists, psychiatrists, or hospital staff. I believe that mental health clinicians and hospital workers do the best they can, in the midst of organizational, financial, and time constraints. In some cases mental health professionals have been essential to a person's survival and recovery. Sadly, in other cases the actions of professionals may re-traumatize a person rather than bringing healing. The problem is larger than the scope of this book.

Statistics. Statistics about the numbers of people in the United States with various brain-based illnesses are seriously flawed. Health professionals generally list a single illness for insurance coding purposes. That may not be an accurate picture of the differences or overlaps between depression, anxiety, post-traumatic stress, ADD, and bipolar spectrum disorders. The problem of labeling is made worse by the format of the Diagnostic and Statistical Manual of Mental Disorders (DSM), published by the American Psychiatric Association.[2] The DSM defines diagnostic criteria for each disorder - including listing grief as a disorder – which does not account for the complexity of human brains and the variation in individual histories.

Statistics about attempted and completed suicides are also flawed, for several reasons. Family members often deny that an individual's emotional pain was extreme enough to cause their death, so death reports may list the death as a single-car accident or a gun malfunction. Though religious views of suicide as a mortal sin are changing, there is still a taboo about talking about the subject. One reason for writing this book is to hear the voices of actual suicide-attempt survivors. Their stories counter false beliefs and assumptions about suicide, and they show the importance of support and resources for anyone trying to move forward into a constructive life.

Language. Researchers, clinicians, and journalists often use words such as "the mentally ill," "he's bipolar," or "she's a schizophrenic." That language adds to the stigma about brain-related problems. I believe that our language choices can either isolate and shame people or open up dialogue and honor their humanity. I avoid calling people "bipolar" or "schizophrenic," but instead talk about them *having* a brain disorder, because these people (and all people) are defined by more than their illness. The stigma attached to the conventional terms for particular brain-based disorders like "bipolar" and "schizophrenic" is only slightly less toxic than words like crazy, nutcase, loony, or just "mental." Negative, stigmatizing language can promote fear, isolation, and ignorance, keeping millions of people from getting the help and support they deserve.

I do not use the terms "mentally ill" or "serious mental illness" in this book, unless used by the person being interviewed. There is no such thing as a mental illness versus a physical illness. These are real health issues, and are not just "in someone's head." All of this happens in the body and in the brain. I choose to use the terms "brain illness" or "brain-based disorder" in this book. Ideally these terms lead us to think about the organ that governs all our actions. "Behavioral health" is widely used but also problematic, since it focuses our attention on observed behaviors, not their source. "Psychiatric disorder" also has stigma-oriented connotations. "Neurobiological disorder" is a mouthful, but it comes closer to conveying the range of brain-based issues people encounter, including autism, ADD, Parkinson's, PTSD, Alzheimer's, and more.

Brain science. The past two decades have given us amazing new knowledge about the brain as a powerful and complex organ. It is the social organ of the body and the determiner of our actions. It is also vulnerable to terrible storms, from inside and outside. Different parts of people's brains can be doing different things at the same time. The research is showing two other facts about human life that have been largely ignored. First, early life experiences have a major impact on how young brains develop. Second, adult brains and behaviors change over time; they depend on many factors, and they exist along a continuum rather than being either "normal" or "abnormal."

Knowledge about the complexities of the brain has grown significantly, but much of that research has not yet reached the general public. Addressing that problem, Daniel Siegel, MD, has provided a helpful image of the brain in the hand, as well as the three key elements affecting our wellbeing: Brain, Mind, and Relationships.[3] Neuroscientist Antonio Damasio has offered evidence that the brain starts with emotion as a guiding force.[4] And Jill Bolte Taylor's experience of a left hemisphere stroke highlights the fact that each brain hemisphere has different and powerful features essential for life.[5]

Audiences. This book is intended for adults of all ages. In particular it is meant to reach three audiences: 1] individuals who may feel alone in their struggle to be healthy and live well in the midst of troubling brain issues; 2] friends, family, and others who want to understand the people they know who have lived through or are living through tsunamis of the mind; and 3] professionals in education, medicine, justice, and faith communities who will benefit from deeper knowledge of their clients' lives and struggles. I trust that *Tsunami of the Mind* will lead them to ask better questions and listen with greater intent, so as to encourage realistic hope for our own and others' futures.

Tsunami of the Mind is at one level simply a book of stories of interesting people. But its intent is more radical. At a time when too many people are ending their lives due to suicidal depression, this book is about changing minds and most of all, saving lives.

INTRODUCTION

THREE TIMES – ONCE in June 1975, once in September 1992, and once in January 2009 – I came close to ending my life by suicide.

Each time I survived, because of close friends, health support, spirituality, and learning more about the brain. Ever since that first near-death experience, I've wanted to figure out what happens to people like me that can leave us desperate and alone, fearing that we can't stand to continue living.

The phrase that emerged as I tried to understand my own and others' frightening experiences is a *tsunami of the mind – the killer waves of suicidal depression.* The question behind this image is one I have asked repeatedly in my own life. How can a person who is often seen as smart, creative, and successful fall into a deep hole of depression that may be invisible to anyone else but is lethal if not addressed?

MY STORY

I grew up in Ohio, a bright but anxious little girl. My mother had depression, and my father drank, but both people were responsible parents raising my two brothers and me. I was quick and verbal in school, but terrified when I played solos in piano recitals. I won honors in high school and college. But as a graduate student at Yale and then at the University of Oregon, the depression I kept hidden in my teens started to overwhelm me. As a doctoral student in Oregon, I was deeply ashamed after the loss of a marriage and the loss of several dear friends who had moved away from Eugene. I was a weak, worthless failure, and I had to stop the pain!

My friend Fran saw me on campus and recognized my lost state. She took me to stay with her and her husband Gordon in Portland. I tried to shake my continuing deadly thoughts while I was there, but it wasn't working. One day I walked away from their apartment and stood above a highway, trying to figure out how I could jump in front of a truck without ending up in the hospital - *alive,* and a *paraplegic!*

A voice came to me as I stood above the highway. *"But Fran and Gordon will be desolate if you go ahead and kill yourself."* "But they s*houldn't* care. <u>*I'm not worth it*</u>!" *"But they do care."* "But they <u>*shouldn't*</u> care about me!" *"But they do."* I don't know how long this went on, and I can't identify the voice as anyone in particular. But I finally turned around and went back to their place and told them I was still desperate and in need of help.

They drove me back to Eugene and connected me with Sue, another close friend. Sue had read up on medicines such as lithium, which was relatively new at that time. I felt okay for a few days, and then my body felt the signal of another fall into desperation and the desire to end it all. Sue went with me to the University of Oregon psychiatrist, trying to find a way to keep me alive. After I told the psychiatrist about my struggles and desperation, he turned to Susan and said, "She can't be manic depressive. She's not extreme enough." But Susan didn't give up. She urged the doctor to consider writing a prescription for lithium. She said to him, "It won't hurt her, and it just might help." He shrugged - I will never forget that shrug! – and then said, "Well, all right - maybe."

TSUNAMI OF THE MIND

Lithium did help me, for sixteen years. I finished my doctorate, taught college, married again, and had a daughter. Over those sixteen years I experienced other life changes, including a second divorce, relocation, and a different job. Then I fell once again into a serious depression. I was driving through Tennessee in June 1992 with my young daughter. I considered driving off the highway to end the pain, but I didn't, because Joanna was with me. Again I knew I was in a desperate state.

I wobbled my way through the next two months. Then, somehow, I found a kind and gifted psychiatrist in Nashville. He saw me through the process of changing medicines while I was briefly in a psychiatric unit. Finally we found a mood-stabilizing medication, oxcarbazepine, which had been used in Europe but was not yet used for bipolar depression in the USA. Along with the antidepressant sertraline and supplements like flaxseed oil and choline, I reemerged as the active, hopeful person I had known myself to be in the past. Once again I survived suicidal depression, with health support, friendship, work I valued, and a loving faith community.

After a messy array of job and personal changes, I moved to rural Washington State in 2002. I became a part-time local pastor for a tiny Methodist Church, where I learned about the National Alliance on Mental Illness, or NAMI.[6] I began sharing my own life struggles with people I trusted in the mental health and faith communities. Living in a rural county along the Pacific coast, I heard about the disturbing number of suicides by local youth and senior citizens in our area. I wanted to see if I could make any difference for other people who were struggling in the communities I had come to love.

I volunteered on the board of the local mental health center, the local NAMI affiliate, and then the state NAMI board. My third close call with suicidal thoughts came while I served as board president for NAMI Washington. A mixture of isolation and heavy criticism led me again into feelings of hopelessness. I escaped from that inner tsunami, but it was a powerful reminder that I was still vulnerable, even though I was doing everything I knew to be healthy and happy.

LISTENING

After I became active as a community mental health advocate, I was asked one day to talk with a young man whose parents feared he would kill himself. After I told the young man about my own near-suicide moments, he promised me he would not hurt himself the next night. Then he challenged me to write down my own story. He said it might help other people who felt alone and afraid, seeing their problem as too strange and too shameful to talk about. I went home and put my Oregon story in writing, but I wasn't sure whether anyone else would want to read it.

For the next several years I listened closely to friends, acquaintances, and friends of friends, "normal" people that you or I might meet and talk with anywhere. Our conversations increasingly went deeper, as I heard about their experiences with alcohol, parental neglect and abuse, serious depression, and attempts at suicide. I realized that these people wanted to know more about people like themselves, not to read more celebrity memoirs. I knew I had gotten through times of suicidal depression. How had other people done that? What happened to turn their stories away from desperation and toward constructive and hopeful lives?

The term "tsunami of the mind" came to me while I was on retreat one January, and it immediately felt true to my own experience. I offered the phrase to people I interviewed over the next four years, and it resonated with them too.

THE STORIES

Each of the ten chapters is based on conversations with someone who, like me, has lived through tsunamis of the mind. The tsunami image helped to encourage dialogue about trauma in their lives and the ways they survived and found support. We talked as peers and friends, and each of us is identified here by actual first name. Most of them live in the Pacific Northwest, but otherwise their backgrounds and stories differ widely.

All ten of these people chose to talk with me without hesitation. They wanted to bring their experience out of the shadows. In some cases that meant looking with new eyes on early troubles, and recognizing the strengths they now bring into their communities, their art, and their relationships. I asked to use their actual first names because I did not want to use pseudonyms. Changing names suggests a reason to hide one's identity, which adds to shame and stigma instead of promoting understanding and recovery.

I am privileged to know these people. Each of them has had an interesting life, as well as terrible experiences. Almost all of them have considered or tried ending their lives at one time or another. But every one of them has a strong desire to live, and each one cares a great deal about the lives of others. We became friends through our stories. I trust you will come to value each of them, as I have done. It is likely that you will learn something from these conversations that opens up a new perspective on your family, your neighbors, your community, or yourself. That is our hope.

BARBARA BATE, PHD

TEN FRIENDS

Beth   Jessie   Mike   Lori   Forrest
Ann   Donna   Jim   Steve   Carol

Every one of these people is a unique individual, with a life that includes positive and negative experiences. In most instances, I first learned of the person because of their struggles. But as we talked, I came to see many other qualities - their determination, creativity, love for family and community, and most of all their resilience.

No one in this book simply fits the commonly used labels of "a mentally ill person" or "suicidal person." They *do* resonate with the phrase that started my journey into writing this book: *tsunami of the mind.* All of them experienced shocks that overwhelmed them, in the midst of what had seemed to them to be normal lives. In some cases, I discovered that what seemed normal to them was not conventional to me, though it made sense in their own experience.

Many of these friends resisted the label "bipolar" when it was first applied to them, given the connotations of manic depression as naked in the street, unpredictably violent, or both. After coming close to suicide, though, they found that a diagnosis of bipolar depression or Bipolar 2 helped put together pieces of their own puzzle, moving them toward hope and recovery. Their experiences are part of the evidence that bipolar depression is more widespread than manic depression (Bipolar 1), although it is not recognized as such by many health professionals and the general public.

I treasure all of these people, especially for their honest sharing of their mistakes and their foibles. None of them blames other people for what has gone wrong in their lives, though many of them have dealt with family and generational problems that added significantly to their problems. Having come close to the edge, they are consistent in showing kindness and compassion toward other people, including strangers.

I want to introduce you to this courageous community of survivors. They have shared a common struggle, each in their own way, and are living into recovery and resiliency. Telling me their stories, with all the rough edges they include, is part of a larger purpose. All of them share with me the desire to bring understanding and compassion into places of pain, confusion, and loss. As my local support group members say, "We will *never* give up *hope!*"

———

BETH

For me, baby steps back to life can begin with appreciating a soft pair of socks, the way the sun shines on trees, or celebrating the fact that I got dressed! If I can string together enough small appreciations, I can get to larger ones and, I believe, so can you.   *- Beth*

BETH AND *I met at a board meeting of NAMI, the National Alliance on Mental Illness, and later at a support group training in 2008. We had this conversation in October 2012. The letter that follows was an email Beth wrote to family and friends the following summer.*

Barb: I've had a vivid image for a number of years: a tsunami of the mind. It's a total experience of body, mind, and spirit. When a tsunami of the mind happens, it's as if everything changes. Energy recedes like ocean waters pulling away from the shore, followed by a huge flood. As we know, the waves in an ocean tsunami can destroy a community. Similarly, a tsunami of the mind is overwhelming, taking away a person's sense of worth and their capacity to think and act in ways that support life.

The question I have asked myself and others is, "How do we keep from losing our lives, when a tsunami of the mind happens?" One possibility is that if you have some warning that an inner tsunami is coming, you have a chance to survive. You can connect with others, move to higher ground, and live through this traumatic event. Understanding how tsunamis of the mind happen is one way to weather them. So I'm asking you and other people I know about your experience.

FAMILY HISTORY

Beth: The logical place to start is a hundred or more years ago, when my grandmother, who didn't have any signs of illness herself, fell in love with my grandfather. He had had a breakdown of some sort in college, and he struggled with depression for the rest of his life. Also, before she met my grandpa, my grandmother's father had killed himself when she was a young adult. So mental illness came from both sides of my mother's family. But I knew none of this when I was growing up.

Barb: So the waters underneath you had a lot hidden in them. You told me earlier that you often stayed at home from school when you were a child. What was happening then?

Beth: We grew up Catholic, in a stable, progressive neighborhood. I was number two of four children. I went to a private Catholic school but stayed home sick quite a bit. I was lactose-intolerant, and it took them a while to figure that out. So I would play fantasy games with my dolls. I was six when Mom was pregnant with a fifth child. I was ecstatic because I was sure this would be a little girl, and she would belong to me. But Mom lost the baby when she was about six months pregnant. The baby things were put away, and nothing more was said. I was devastated.

Barb: That must have been a shock for you.

Beth: It was difficult. They were Catholic, so there was no birth control. And my mother had grown up with a depressive father. From the age of eleven or twelve, all I wanted was to be a mom. My job was to get a man, and be a mom! By eighth grade, I was in public school and playing that role with my friends. That's where I met Tom, my first husband. We dated for a few weeks, went our separate ways, and then after high school we decided to get married. Tom was going to school in Spokane, so I moved over there to join him.

Barb: So your dream was coming true.

Both: I thought so at first, but things went haywire in Spokane after a few months, so we came back to Seattle. I worked for a small company whose offices were in the family home. That family had gone to Hawaii for Christmas, so the other office manager and I were left in charge. The oldest son of the family was on disability, and we knew he did a lot of drugs. While the family was away, he called the office and demanded that we give him money. We didn't, but the other office manager went home, and I was there alone. I was nineteen and very naïve. Someone claiming to be the son's doctor called, saying that the son was threatening to kill himself if we didn't give him money. I didn't give him money, but I did call the police to request a welfare check.

Over Christmas, my husband Tom and I went to a Christmas party. I was very worried about my employer's son, but had no way to get any information. I felt very odd, so I went home alone. At home, reality disappeared. I was listening to the radio and heard the DJ say he was talking with a guy threatening to kill himself. I became sure that he was talking about my employer's son, or about my ex-boyfriend or my brother-in-law.

HOSPITAL

That night I was trying to clean the apartment because my in-laws were coming to visit the next day. I thought I was cleaning, but in fact I dumped out every drawer and cupboard. When my husband came home after the party, I was sitting on the bed in hysterics. He called my mother, and they took me to the psychiatric hospital, where I stayed for about two weeks. I recall the employers being robbed, the FBI coming to investigate, and my being questioned while in the hospital. But as I look back, I still have no idea what was real and what was not.

Barb: But you know now that you were not well.

Beth: Yes. While I was in the hospital, my husband quit the job for me, or they fired me; I have no idea which. When I got out of the hospital, I simply couldn't stay in my apartment. I was overwhelmed, and I threatened to kill myself unless I could go home to my parents' house for a while.

My parents found a clubhouse, where I could be with other people during the day. I also started seeing a therapist named Mike. The first day I went in, Mike asked that my whole family come in, everybody who lived at home, and my husband Tom. After everyone else went in, I went in and said, 'Hi, I'm the patient." He winked and said, "Don't be too sure."

[Both laugh.]

Beth: After having been in the hospital, I had many symptoms. I typed up all the symptoms in a list, and I took the list to the psychiatrist I was seeing. He handed me a drug interaction sheet, and all of my symptoms were on it. So I flushed the drugs and fired the doctor. Since Tom and I needed income, I found a new job and went back to work.

Tom and I went to Mike for quite a while. Two years after my breakdown, Tom decided it was time to leave, because he was gay. It was good that I had the support of my therapist then. I was mortified about my breakdown, filled with shame, and I still didn't know any of the family history. I wanted to make it up to my family for what I'd done to them.

Barb: What do you remember about your ups and downs during that time?

Beth: Looking back, my perception is that I just went under. I did whatever anyone expected of me. I didn't trust my own volition, because I'd had an illness, and I had no peer support, even though the counselor was trying to build my self-esteem. My parents by then had moved to Pennsylvania. So I moved in with different friends and dated a lot of men, because I needed to affirm my femininity. Also I was date raped. It was a relative of a relative, the first and last time I ever saw him. That was complicated and painful, but like many things in my life I didn't really process it until many years later.

PENNSYLVANIA

My parents were living in Pittsburgh by then. I didn't like my job at a medical supply firm, and I wanted to go to college. Mom and Dad said that they'd help, if I could get back there. So I got there, under unusual circumstances. While I was married to Tom, we were at a party and met another couple. She had gone to the same high school as I had. The four of us, Tom and I and Jerry and his wife, did everything together while Tom and I were married. So when Tom left, it seemed natural for me to lean on Jerry. But I needed too much at that point. Wanting to reaffirm my femininity, I had a brief affair with Jerry when he came to Seattle for training.

One reason I decided to go to Pennsylvania was that I wasn't going to wreck Jerry's marriage. I didn't think that Jerry wanted that either. So I called Jerry one day and said," I'm moving to Pennsylvania; want to give me a ride?" I was kidding! But both Jerry and his wife called back a little while later. She was pregnant with their first child, and they said, "This is probably our last chance to travel. So okay, we'll give you a ride."

[Both chuckle.]

Beth: So the three of us drove to Pennsylvania! While living there, I went to community college for a couple of years, had several boyfriends and relationships, and big ups and downs. I lived with my parents the first year, until they moved back to Washington State.

Barb: Why had they gone to Pennsylvania?

Beth: It was for Dad's work, but he got laid off soon after I got there, so they had no money to help me through college. I qualified for community college and I got loans, so I did it on my own. I changed colleges, changed men, and changed jobs. When anything got uncomfortable, I had to make a major change! After three different colleges, I graduated with my bachelor's degree in English literature, with departmental honors.

HUSBAND JOE

I wanted to be a teacher, but I couldn't afford to do the grad school, so I went to work for a law firm. Then Joe, my second husband, came along. He was a drug addict and an alcoholic, but he was clean when we got married.

Barb: Was he fun?

Beth: Great fun. He was delightful! He was younger than me, and he'd never really grown up. During the two years we were married I had dark depressions, and I wanted to move home. Joe and I came west for one visit, and then went back to Pittsburgh. Neither of us was making a lot of money. We smoked pot and did a fair amount of drinking, but I managed to keep my jobs. I always did well at my jobs, so it was easy to get another one. But I knew I was getting further from my purpose in life, whatever that was.

I saw a therapist in Pennsylvania for a number of years. The therapist finally said to me that he wouldn't see me individually anymore, since we were not making any progress. But he said he would see me in a group. I went to the group, still trying to prove something to the therapist, but I would cry my way home afterwards. I had to quit therapy, because I couldn't afford it on my own.

After Joe started using drugs again, he became unpredictable. I finally decided to leave him, after he had put his fist through the dashboard of my car when we were driving. He also wrecked the car in the snow one night, when he was driving stoned.

Barb: Were you scared?

Beth: Somehow I knew that he would never hurt me, but I was scared for us, since we were driving when it happened. I was also thinking it was his fault that my life was not going well. His family had become my whole life, so when I divorced him, I had to give them up. I was essentially alone for a year before I came back to Washington. And I was diagnosed with systemic lupus that year, so I became very depressed and planned suicide for the first time.

Barb: How were you going to do it?

Beth: With pills. I had all kinds of antidepressants, and I'd saved up the pain pills from dental work and other things. I was going to take all of them. I didn't know then that nine times out of ten, that doesn't kill the person. In the middle of that night, I called my friend Mary Ann, who is

Joe's sister and was my friend before he was. She didn't know how to handle my call, so she said "Don't be silly, go back to bed." So I did!

Barb: Do you think she didn't believe you?

Beth: Possibly not. I thought some more about all this, and I realized I needed to go back home where people could support me. My college friends in Pittsburgh had all moved on. So I did a lot of financial finagling, and I wound up back in the Northwest.

Barb: What did you do to get back here? Did you steal? [Laughing]

Beth: Oh, no! I was a Catholic Girl Scout, always honest to a fault. I just went to a car dealer and said, "I need a car, and I can only afford to pay two hundred dollars a month. I don't care what kind it is as long as it can get me to the west coast." The only thing they said I could qualify for was a brand new car, because my credit was not good. The logic there eludes me.

BACK HOME

So I had a brand new car! My brother flew from the Northwest to Pittsburgh, and we drove back together. I shipped all my stuff on a train, after packing it all in the middle of Pittsburgh humidity. It took a couple of months to go across the states, and when I opened it up, everything was mildewed and most of it had to be thrown away.

I started by staying with my parents in the Seattle area, but the only job I could find was in Portland, Oregon. So I moved there. That was the start of another downward slide. I didn't have any support system around me except for my grandmother, who was severely judgmental.

Barb: Did you live with her?

Beth: No. I got an apartment right away, but I was frequently at her house. That was difficult. At times we were friends, and at other times not. My job in Portland was similar to the job I had loved in Pittsburgh, as office manager for an accounting firm. The first few months were good, but then a woman who had been on leave came back, and she wanted her job back. I had no solid sense of myself. I was Jell-O at the core. So I just quit, and I lost all my benefits. One thing that was constructive this time is that I talked to my boss about my stress. While the boss was somewhat sympathetic, she was not aware of my having any mental health issues, and there was no Employee Assistance Program to refer me to.

When the Portland job ended, I had to stop seeing the therapist I had seen, and find a new therapist. During all these years, I'd been on various antidepressants. I'd get an antidepressant, and I would get the lovely and delightful high. Then I'd stop taking the pills when I felt good, and crash into the depths of depression. That happened while I was in Portland.

Barb: So your therapists weren't your prescribers, and you would get medications from your primary care provider?

Beth: Yes. The primary care provider always went with the choice that I had depression, not bipolar disorder, even though I told them I had an initial diagnosis of bipolar disorder.

Barb: For many years, the majority of primary care doctors didn't know about bipolar depression, and many still do not recognize different types of bipolar illness.

JOBS

Beth: Yes, that's what I've found. In any case, Mom and Dad helped me get back on my feet financially, and I found a job at Hewlett Packard. One day I was driving up to Skagit County with a friend, and I learned that Jerry and his wife had split. I stopped by the house and left a note, since he wasn't home. Jerry called me that night, and we reconnected. That meant another big change. I moved from Vancouver, Washington, up to Everett.

I went to see an MD in Everett, who said, "You're not bipolar; you're not running naked in the streets!" I reported to him the previous psychotic episode from years earlier, when I thought the radio was talking to me. He still said, "No; just take these pills." And he did not offer me the option of going to a psychiatrist.

Barb: He said, "Just take these antidepressants?"

Beth: Yes. Just go to the pharmacy and take these antidepressants. In the meantime, I followed up with other doctors on my lupus diagnosis, and I had that overturned. But I found I did have fibromyalgia and other related conditions, so I looked for and found alternative treatments.

In my next job, I was manager of information services at Internet Technologies, a worldwide corporation in Everett. People reported to me from three different states, and I was traveling a lot. I was extremely stressed. Every time I explained to my boss that I was stressed, they would expand my department or give me a raise, or both. Finally I just cracked.

JERRY AND KIDS

In the meantime, I had married Jerry, and we had his two kids with us for much of the time. They were a girl fourteen and a boy of ten, and they were not happy about having a stepmother. I on the other hand was thrilled, because I never could have children.

Barb: How did you know that?

Beth: I was diagnosed with polycystic ovarian syndrome just before I left for Pittsburgh. I was thrilled years later to be married to Jerry, and to have his children in my life. I was pie-eyed about getting a chance to be a parent, but they were not. Their mother lived very close, so it was decided that Ashley would stay with her mom and Aaron would stay with us. Every day after school they both went to their mom's house. They also had every other weekend together. With the kids and the jobs and the drives back and forth, the stress and tension were extreme. I had another physical and mental break, crying and shaking, and unable to go to work or even talk. I lay on the couch in my pajamas for days.

Barb: What happened with Aaron at that point?

Beth: When I broke, Jerry sent Aaron to be with his mom for a while. I felt responsible for the destruction of the family. Because I couldn't work, we wouldn't be able to pay for the kids' college. It was devastating. I finally found a wonderful psychiatrist who would treat me, and he was supportive of the bipolar diagnosis. He prescribed the meds for me that got me going in a better direction.

Still, I was looking for more. So I went to see a naturopath and started on a gluten-free, wheat-free, dairy-free diet. I went down to a hundred and nine pounds, was sickly, and had a huge amount of body pain. I still had no faith in myself, so when my psychiatrist told me to go to a NAMI support group, I went! It was a support group that is for both consumers and family members. Jerry and I went there for quite a long time.

UNITY

Another important healing began in 2001, when I went with two friends to a meditation chapel in the woods. At first there was singing, then silent meditation. I was bouncing off the walls, in effect, with tears streaming down my face, from the effort to hold still. All of a sudden I heard a voice saying, "Go to Unity in Mount Vernon." What?? It was an audible voice. I went home, and I said to my husband, "We have to go to this Church of Unity, because I got this message." I've been going there ever since.

Beginning on that spiritual path has been critical to my recovery. I felt I was starting to get my feet under me again. What kept coming up in meditations was wanting to teach other people to be more stable in their mental health, and to understand about mental health issues, not to ignore them. When the NAMI Peer to Peer program came along, it was just perfect. Someone had already written it!

I was asked at a support group if I'd like to be trained for the Peer to Peer course, and I immediately said "Yes!" My NAMI affiliate sent me to Mississippi for Peer to Peer state mentor training. I became a state trainer, and then I was asked to do state trainings in other areas. Then NAMI hired me to work for the new NAMI Connection Recovery Support Group program at the national level. That meant long hours and a huge amount of travel. Again, it was huge stress, and I couldn't handle it. For a person with high standards, that meant killing myself!

Barb: I know you have given more than 100% to this NAMI work. Having it relate so closely to your own experience made it even more taxing personally. I think we've been through some of the same big waves. We have wanted to be healers, and to bring support to others as well as getting support for ourselves.

Beth: Yes. Empathy is basic to my being.

Barb: You told me earlier about being a foster parent for a time. How did that happen, and what did you know or not know when he came to you?

FOSTERING

Beth: We read Kyle's file before we met him. He was nine years old, and he had suffered horrendous abuse at the hands of his parents, his uncle, and his siblings. He hadn't known anything but abuse. When we met him, he was the most adorable, pleasant child I could imagine. We agreed overnight to take him, rather than having a number of visits over time. The first three months were great. We all thoroughly enjoyed each other.

Then he had his first terrible tantrum. We were terribly concerned that he was a danger to himself and others at that moment, since Jerry couldn't contain him physically. So we called the police, and they handled it beautifully. But how many times are you going to have the police coming to your house? During the tantrum, Kyle looked at Jerry and said, "This is the real me." Kyle had been holding it all in all that time.

My heart just opened to Kyle in a big way, and we worked hard to form a relationship with him. What that meant for me was to drive him to therapy, to karate, and to school. He had to be supervised 24-7. He couldn't be alone with any other child or adult. So it was difficult - - a high level of stress, punctuated by these terrible tantrums. Because of the way he was raised, Kyle had no respect for women, so the only time I felt safe was when Jerry was home. But I was alone with Kyle the majority of time. I was getting sicker and sicker, but I didn't realize it. When I went to the school, I felt like the oddball mom who didn't fit in.

Barb: It sounds as if you didn't have any structure or safety for yourself in the midst of this. You were in *charge*, and at *risk*, all the time.

Beth: That's exactly it. One time we were driving back home from therapy, and I don't know why, but he made a huge crack in the dash, and nearly broke the window out of the car. Another time, he was throwing around a huge piece of cardboard, and it went right in front of my face as I was driving. I didn't know whether or not to stop the car, which would have put him out on the freeway if he got out. So I just kept driving, white-knuckling it all the way.

Barb: I'm thinking of something a friend told me many years ago when I visited her in New York City. She was a social work student in southeast Manhattan. When we passed a homeless man on the sidewalk, I asked her, "How do you deal with this?" She said, "I remind myself that in some cases it's one to one. If I deal with this one person, it will take all of me, and I wouldn't be able to help anyone else."

Beth: Toward the end of the time with Kyle, I was stressed to the max again, and I was hospitalized. After I came out of the hospital, I said to Jerry, "I just can't have this boy in my life." It crushed both of us, and it nearly wrecked our marriage. Jerry loves children above all else. When he came home from dropping Kyle off, he literally collapsed into tears on the floor. I will never forget that.

We have kept in touch with Kyle over the years. We've been like grandparents to him, going to all his events. He's almost eighteen now, and he's been through many more homes. He's having a rough life.

Barb: Some time ago you told me about a book you have, *Empowered by Empathy*,[7] which describes many different types of empathy. I remember being struck by the statement that empathy can be costly.

Beth: Yes. I believe that part of the terrific stress I felt was that I was picking up on Kyle's chaotic emotions.

Barb: Given the person you are, I don't see how you could avoid that. I think we both struggle to maintain the first part of the phrase "detachment with love." We need to have compassion for the other, without swallowing their feelings and then falling down ourselves! It's not easy to do.

Beth: Yes, detachment with love sounds good – and it can be hard to manage.

I was hospitalized while we had Kyle, then after I left NAMI, and then again last summer. I had gotten a little bit back on my feet, and then I slid backwards. I don't know exactly what triggered this, but I spent all of last summer in my backyard, feeling very suicidal.

BETH"S EMAIL

Barb: I remember the email you sent to your whole email list last summer. My sense was that you felt you were hanging on by baby toothpicks, saying, "I would like *not* to want to kill myself. I would like to *want* to be alive. But I have no idea how to get across this chasm."

Beth: It was like that for me. I got an amazing number of responses to that email, including from people I hadn't heard from in ages. There was so much support from everyone, while I was feeling so alone. I had the deep dark depressions and the high wire stress sensations, all at the same time.

Right now I think that we've finally gotten my meds to where they work and contain the anxiety edge. That has been tremendous. For the third year, I've been working at the crisis center, five hours a day, four days a week. And I am able to do my workshops on the side. I was actually thinking today that I might even try fulltime work. But the circumstances have to be just right.

Barb: I've heard you at your workshops, especially your Courageous Communication workshop. It's clear to me that you like and are good at that work. You nourish other people.

Beth: I would like that work to be enough to make a living. But that may just be a way that I give back.

Barb: In my own life, office jobs have never been a good fit. Sitting still is hard! Right now the mix that works for me is doing music, mental health advocacy, and writing. Some people say to me, "Oh, you're so busy!" But it doesn't seem that way to me. I get to do one thing I like to do, then another thing I like, and I take a break or switch to something else, when I get stuck or need a change.

Beth: How long did it take you to find that place?

Barb: [Laughs] All my life! As I look back at my teaching and writing over the years, I have always loved stories, interviewing people, and writing words that are true and hopeful. What both of us are doing right now is creative and possibility-oriented. In the scheme of the universe, either of us could be sitting in either seat today.

Beth: I can see that. I used to fancy myself a writer, but writing is hard work!

Barb: It certainly can be. But it's a funny thing. I taught speech communication for years, but then I had a mini-stroke in the speech performance area of my brain. I still have times when I can't get the right word out in conversation. But when I get stressed while writing, I leave the computer, eat an almond or a carrot, and then come back to try it again.

Beth: I like that idea. I may take my workshops and make them into a book at some point.

I thought of two other things I want to add. The first is from my most recent hospital experience. I left APA (against physician's advice) and my reason was that the place was a totally chaotic environment. I couldn't stay there! The point I want to make is that people with our kind of illness really need a place of *order and quiet* in order to heal.

The second experience has to do with the church I decided to attend. I was talking with one of the two ministers, when she said, "There's no such thing as mental illness."

Barb: Oooh! That statement was effectively denying your experience.

Beth: Right. So I found literature from NAMI FaithNet[8] and took it with me to talk to the minister. We chewed on it quite a lot, and finally I said, "If I was born with no legs, you would not be asking me to kneel in prayer. I see this as the same thing." So my message to others is that there *is* such a thing as a mental illness, and not to devalue what anyone else has lived through.

Barb: I will add to this some comments made by Dr. Tom Insel at the 2012 NAMI national convention in Seattle.[9]

Beth: Who is he?

Barb: He is the psychiatrist who directs NIMH, the National Institute of Mental Health. He speaks at the NAMI convention each year about current brain research. At his most recent talk, he first showed us information about the percentages of improvement in our knowledge about heart disease and cancer. There's been a tremendous increase in life expectancy for people with both heart disease and cancer, but not a major improvement in the field of mental health. He stated that our record over the past four or five decades is not great. "We need to know much more about the brain." For many of the medications that are prescribed currently, the outcomes are much more unpredictable than people are led to believe. When asked if a given medicine will work with a given person, he said, "We *don't know that.*"

Dr. Insel made another statement to the NAMI leaders and members that resonated with me. He said that the language we are using is problematic. His organization is the National Institute of *Mental* Health and NAMI is the National Alliance on *Mental* Illness. But the word 'mental' is not serving us well. These are *brain illnesses*. They are based in the brain, the central organ of the body. So choosing not to use the word *brain* is misleading.

Personally, I've been bothered by another widely used term, *behavioral health*. When you say Behavioral Health, it sounds like the issue is behavior. "Just behave right and things will be fine." Not at all! There are many levels of what happens inside a person that can affect behavior, including our DNA, chromosomes, brain circuitry, and so forth.

Beth: I agree that phrase is misleading. But I always assumed that it was named behavioral health because we could go there to learn new behaviors to help with our health.

Barb: That's a positive way to look at it. But too often I hear words like "You're a bad kid" or "He's never held a job" or "She's just too emotionally needy." A lot of factors are in play, but the brain is *always* part of it. You and I didn't *make* our own brains.

Beth: And I have the family history to prove it! [Both chuckle.]

Barb: I've been thinking about the part of that tsunami of the mind image, the invisible parts of what happens beneath the ocean. Your family history is a great example of that.

Beth: And much of that history eventually helped me to see that my genetic background was loaded with brain disorders, as you put it.

The secrecy over the generations influenced me to believe that everyone else was *fine*, and *I* was the problem, *just me*. My current psychiatrist is helpful, because he knows that he doesn't know everything, and he is happy to work with all the alternative ideas I bring. That's huge!

Barb: That's the ideal, as I see it, the two of you working together. I also have a prescriber who works with me. And when other people ask me how I keep going as I do, I tell them I'm a health nut! A lot of things affect my wellbeing: specific vitamins and supplements and the medications I take, exercise, journaling, my dog, reading and films, and meditation, when I remember to do it!

I want to go back to the matter of knowing more about the brain. I watched Charlie Rose's program on the brain the other night. Brain surgeon Dr. Helen Mayberg talked about her microsurgeries with patients who had treatment-resistant depression. She described the response made by one surgery patient, who was conscious as the tiny electrode was being activated in area 25 of his brain. He said aloud, "Oh, I feel so much lighter; what did you do??" [10] That's a fascinating true story. I hope we'll hear more of those accounts in the future.

Beth: I hope so too. I went into the care center the other day, and I said, "I do not know how people work here fulltime!"

Barb: The people I know who are good therapists don't have our brain circuitry. Or if they do, they have found some circuit-breakers.

Beth: Circuit-breaker is perfect. Have you heard of the research reports about ketamine?

Barb: Is that the one that brings an almost immediate release from deep depression?

Beth: Yes. Its side effects can be hallucinations, so it's tricky. But it can be the start of a whole new class of medications.

Barb: It's appropriate that our conversation is turning toward possibilities. I believe your own story, Beth, will open up possibilities for other people too. Thank you!

The summer after our October conversation, Beth sent the following email to her family and friends. It is included here, condensed, with Beth's permission.

To my Dearest Family, including my dearest friends who were chosen rather than given. Both are a gift from the Universe.

There is a song called "We Are All Angels" that contains the lyrics "We are all angels who only have one wing. We need each other to fly."

I am emerging from my latest bout of devastating depression. It has slowly dawned on me again how much pain this illness causes all of you. Did you know that our Great, Great, Great Grandfather had "hallucinations that unfit him for business?" Or that our Great Grandfather took his own life? Did you know that our own Grandfather went regularly for what were known as shock treatments? There are other genetic examples but our forefathers and mothers didn't have the information or the skill to talk about it, so it was held as an embarrassing secret – a character flaw.

Much of the time I am working to make the small choices that keep me well, but sometimes I simply have no choice;

the darkness rules. My hope is that spreading this knowledge will make it safe for people with bipolar disorder or other illnesses to ask for help, to talk it out and to help each other. I do not support suicide as a rational choice, and yet I know that the illness sometimes takes away my ability to be rational.

I have created a safety plan for baby-stepping back into life. The challenge comes in deciding to take those first baby steps, knowing after 30 years of living with this illness that the darkness will inevitably return. I am strong in the sense that I can be there for others, even in the darkness. It is good for me to help others. It reminds me that I can help myself. Please do not protect me from what goes on in your lives because you perceive me to be fragile.

My baby steps back to life begin with such things as appreciating a soft pair of socks, the way the sun shines on trees, or celebrating the fact that I got dressed! If I can string together enough small appreciations, I can get to larger ones, and I believe, so can you. This illness has become more devastating with every bout. You can help by simply being real with me. I am stronger than I seem.

Knowledge and hope are a powerful combination. If you would like more knowledge about the illness, check out NAMI at www.nami.org or Mental Health America at www. mha.org. Or ask me, and I will tell you what I know.

Please feel free to share this with anyone who might appreciate it.

JESSIE

My son gave a speech in May when I walked the stage at graduation. "I am proud of my mom; she took a class called 'stats.' I don't know what it is, but it made her cry. She has to take a lot of medication, but I'm so happy that she's the best mom ever."   **- Jessie**

JESSIE AND I met through a mutual friend in Spokane. Both women were active in the local NAMI affiliate. This conversation took place in December 2012.

Jessie: When you first contacted me about these interviews, I thought, "Here's a woman who's putting people's stories on paper as a way to advocate for better understanding. I need to meet her."

Barb: I appreciate your coming to talk with me, Jessie. We haven't met before today, but I believe we have some experiences in common. I wrote down some general questions that refer to how it can feel to a person to experience what I call a tsunami of the mind. I'm curious about how people survive and move beyond those experiences. What occurs to you may come from any of a number of directions. Not everyone wants to talk about things like suicide, alcoholism, or family situations. So feel free to say what makes sense to you to share.

I'll give you some background from my own life. In my teens I was active and feeling okay much of the time, but at other times I was depressed and unable to sleep at night. Years later, when I was in doctoral study and considering suicide, I got lifesaving help when a friend took me to the University psychiatrist and advocated for me. The psychiatrist said to my friend, "She can't be manic depressive. She's not extreme enough." With my friend's urging, the doctor wrote a prescription for lithium, and that medicine worked well for me for many years.

Jessie: I've known doctors who don't ask enough questions when someone comes to see the doctor about being depressed. They don't try to see if there's something behind that. When people don't see the bigger story and don't listen for it, they just ask about behaviors and they use a set of written criteria from the DSM (Diagnostic and Statistical Manual of Mental Disorders). That's just not enough.

Barb: I agree!

IN HER TEENS

Jessie: My own symptoms started when I was fourteen or fifteen. I think they were triggered by trauma and alcoholism that happened at home. Being Hispanic just made things very difficult. My mom denied my experience of depression at that point. She took me to a neurologist, because in my culture you don't go to psychiatrists. I had my first suicide attempt when I was fifteen, my second at seventeen, and my third when I was twenty-one.

Barb: You didn't complete those attempts. That's a good thing!

Jessie: Each time they would give me antidepressants. It would make me feel good for a little while, a month or so, and then it would send me tumbling again. I had read somewhere that when the neurotransmitter serotonin acts up, you feel different. So until I was in my early thirties, whenever I felt strange I thought that my serotonin must be doing something odd. But there were other rumblings under the water that were not visible at first. I have a cousin who passed away last January who has schizophrenia. We think my dad has bipolar disorder and my mom certainly has depression. So I think there's definitely something hereditary going on.

I did well in school, regardless of everything. I was very creative, very social, and then this hit me. It was like invisible ninjas attacking me, and I wasn't sure what was going on. Sometimes I would just take off walking until I couldn't walk any more, trying to get away from those feelings.

I was married when I was nineteen, and divorced when I was twenty one. He's a wonderful person, but we were young and it was the right thing to divorce. I went back home to the state where I'm from. I made another attempt, or quasi-attempt, to kill myself. Then my mother took me to a military hospital.

While I was in the hospital they told me I had a visitor. My mom had come to bring me clothes. Right behind my mom I could see this man who was clutching a little teddy bear. I was mortified! I thought, "Omigosh, do you know that you're in a loony bin?" I actually said it. "Are you aware that the people here are not okay?" He said, "Yes, I'm aware. But you seem like a person I want to get to know." He wasn't fazed. That is the person who's now my husband. To this day, almost thirteen years later, it's a little unnerving that it doesn't faze him.

When I was released they again gave me antidepressants. They also gave me medicines for anxiety, and I became dependent on them. Thirteen years later I am still trying to wean myself off of the anti-anxiety medications.

Barb: They didn't give you any of the medicines known as mood stabilizers?

Jessie: No. The psychologist there mentioned the B word, asking if I was bipolar. I said to her "No, I'm not crazy. Go to hell!"

HUSBAND AND CHILDREN

One reason I talk about my husband when I tell my story is that even without a diagnosis, somebody accepted me. He saw the bigger picture, and saw beyond whatever was going on with me. I know I said to him, "I'm complicated. Life with me has never been easy for anyone, including myself. Are you actually going to stick around?" He said "Yes." My husband is white, not Hispanic, so both of us have had culture shock.

We have two children together, a boy and a girl. In 2005 my little girl was diagnosed with autism. The doctors speculate that some of the genes that cause bipolar disorder are also involved in autism. My son, who's twelve, has ADHD (attention deficit hyperactivity disorder) and may also have bipolar Type Two. People often ask me, "How to you feel about that?" I could feel responsible, or I could dissect my children, but that wouldn't do anybody any good. My daughter has big curly hair like I do. She also has a great sense of humor, as I do. So I'm blessed that I have my children. I wouldn't trade them for the world.

If it happens that my son has a bipolar problem, I hope I will know enough to give him the skills and support he needs. I'm pretty transparent with him, sharing on a need to know basis. I let him see me when I do well and also when I don't do so well. If any of those things happens to my children or their children, I want them to have whatever knowledge they need.

RED SHOES AND MUSIC BOXES

I am thirty-five now. When I was thirty or thirty-one, I woke up one morning and knew that I needed to get red shoes. I *had* to have red shoes. It was winter. Exactly eleven days from now is the anniversary of that day.

Barb: You remember that exact day?

Jessie: Oh yes! I sat in front of stores waiting for them to open. I felt like they weren't opening fast enough. I needed those shoes, *now*. I went to several stores and couldn't find the right shade of red shoes. I spent about five hundred dollars from our rent on red shoes. It was like being in a movie. Someone had turned up the volume on everything sensory, everything I could see or smell or feel. I had felt that way before, but I didn't know that was hypomania (elevated mood, fast speech, and intensity of ideas and actions).

The night after the shoe incident, I remember I was feeling very creative. So the next day I decided to go music box shopping. I went to thrift stores and collected broken music boxes, ones where the outsides were damaged. I was intent on taking out the music mechanism and putting the music mechanism from each of them into its rightful container.

Barb: That was an amazing idea.

SUPERWOMAN

Jessie: Also during this episode I went to Wal-Mart, and for the first time in my life I shoplifted, a lipstick. Three days later I hooked up with somebody I knew, and we had a sexual relationship for about a month. My husband and kids didn't know about any of this. They did know that I tend to be mercurial. In my own head everything was making perfect sense. I didn't have to sleep or eat. I was sexy and smart, like Superwoman.

During those days I felt like I was surfing, able to cruise big huge-ass waves! I didn't know they were going to come crashing down on me.

Barb: Were you taking any medicine or medicines at that point?

Jessie: I was taking the anti-anxiety pills and the sleeping pills, but not the anti-depressants. I know now that I was physiologically hooked on those medicines.

Barb: Who was providing your medicines at that point? Did you have a primary care physician, a psychiatrist, or what?

Jessie: The person who diagnosed me was a therapist who worked for a nonprofit. I hadn't ever seen a psychiatrist, because I didn't have private insurance. Then and now I go to a public clinic, where I see a psychiatric registered nurse practitioner. She talks with me about meds and gets the prescriptions arranged through a physician's assistant (PA) who doesn't know me personally. I have done my own research with a lot of the medicines that I take.

After the episode I told you about, I said to the nurse practitioner, "Something's wrong with me." I've always had insight when something was wrong. This time I knew that something was *really wrong*. She said, "You meet all of the criteria for bipolar disorder, type two."

BIPOLAR TYPE TWO

The nurse practitioner knew I had all these depressions and the hypomania, and suddenly this manic episode. So she sent me to the doctor. They gave me lithium, which helped, but I couldn't pay for all the blood tests that were required. So I tried Depakote and it made me really sick. Then they put me on lamotrigine, Lamictal, and it was good. They also put me on a little bit of risperidone, which is an antipsychotic, plus the two other medicines I was on. Prior to this I had been self-medicating with alcohol along with my meds.

Barb: Was the alcohol to help you be calmer?

Jessie: Mostly I was seeking sleep. I never had a psychotic break, but I was often uncomfortable and irritable, so I mixed the meds with Benadryl and alcohol at night. Eventually I was able to stop self-medicating, but now and forever I can't have Benadryl in my house. With lamotrigine and risperidone and the two others, I was able to come down to earth.

Then it was time to fess up. "Omigosh, I have to tell my husband everything!" And I did. He is a man of grace, and he forgave me. He said, "Okay, we need to figure this out." I'm an academic person, so I bought a lot of books and said to myself, "I'll find the answers. I need to know everything I can about this thing that keeps attacking me."

Also during this time my thinking became completely unraveled. I thought to myself, "My husband is a very good-looking person. What if I was manic or hypomanic and I married him for his looks? Or what if I didn't really want to have children, but I made that decision because I was depressed?" I started picking apart my life and asking myself, "How much of this was Jessie's decision, and how much was the disorder's decision?"

Two years after being stable, through therapy and the right medications, my husband asked me to re-marry him. He said, "Okay, you're now stable and you can make that choice."

Barb: Wow.

Jessie: Yes. His continuous support is something else!

COLLEGE

Slowly I started getting things together in my life. I knew I wanted to go to college. I was able to go to a private liberal arts college with the help of a full year's tuition. I'm a psychology major, which is appropriate for me. I had to make my professors aware of my disorder, because sometimes it would slow me down or stop me in my tracks.

One of the unfortunate things about my experience with bipolar disorder – and I know that other people who have Type Two also experience it – is mixed episodes. To me those are the real tsunamis of the mind! When you're really depressed, you just don't act; you're lethargic. And if you're manic you can do something stupid, often inadvertently. But mixed episodes are confusing. It feels like you're in this giant washing machine.

Barb: Or maybe a centrifuge?

Jessie: Yes. You're tumbling and tumbling. I remember one time I was bodysurfing in Mazatlan. I got caught in an undercurrent while I was tethered to the board. I was able to get up to the top because my board floated up to the surface. But I remember distinctly that feeling of being rolled under and under!

MIXED EPISODES

A mixed state is something that is huge for my family, for this is the only state that I can't recognize when it happens. It's saying, "I don't feel right." As soon as my husband, my mom, or my mentors hear it, I go "Wow." That is the time to brace myself. The problem with mixed episodes – with bipolar disorder in general, but especially mixed episodes – is that *you know* they're coming. If you have enough insight you can tell that they're coming but there's not a damn thing you can do about it. You can take meds that will slow them down, or once you're there they can help stop it. But it's *there*, and it's coming. It's that ominous fear, knowing that it's coming. . . . I think that's even worse than when it actually gets there. And then the aftermath is tremendous.

I have to buy medications out of pocket since I don't have insurance,. This last year was really hard. My husband was laid off and I was trying to finish school and we barely made ends meet. So every time they switched my meds I had to pay for the new one. And then falling behind in school was devastating. I've always been a good student, and there were high expectations of me. I gained a total of sixty-two pounds. I'm five feet four inches tall, and I'm pushing two hundred four pounds!

Barb: And many of the medicines have an effect on your weight.

Jessie: That's devastating for me. I've always been a thin, petite person. Some of the medications I take slow down my metabolism or make me very hungry. Some people tell me, "Well, you have to have enough self-control." I say, "When you want to stay alive and raise your children and do what you've got to do, you've got to put some things in the back."

Barb: Those are terrible choices. I know that some clinicians say, "Weight gain just goes with the territory; that's just how it is." But that is not fair! Other people with serious illnesses don't have to deal with side effects that can lead to diabetes, heart disease and strokes.

Jessie: Yes, it is unfair. I'm going to live with this for the rest of my life. How? I'm a Christian. I believe in God. And sometimes I think, "Lord, you overestimate me, really you do, because I don't know that I can live with this." About five weeks ago I was very, very sick. I hit another bottom after many years of doing okay. I thought to myself, "I don't know if I can pull out of this." I know it was triggered by situations that just aggravated it. I feel better now, but that recent experience is still vivid.

RECOVERY

I'm an officer of the local National Alliance on Mental Illness affiliate. I go around town and give presentations about recovery. I also facilitate a support group, and we talk about recovery there. But how do you talk about recovery when it's something chronic? For me it's something very personal. With things like tsunamis, they are natural disasters. This tsunami of the mind is a natural disaster too! It is a medical condition we have no control over. And what little control we have is often misused, either because of the disorder or because we don't have the resources to exercise the control we do have.

Barb: You're right.

Jessie: A lot of times it means that you have to live in a bubble. You can't be stressed, you have to exercise, and you have to go to bed early. It's a natural disaster, this disorder, and the cleanup costs can be incredible. People on the outside don't realize what it costs.

People often talk about in-groups and out-groups. Whether people like it or not we have an us versus them in relation to mental illnesses. The very first time I came to a group of people who have to live with a mental illness, I heard people saying, "You can't be here unless you have a mental illness."

Barb: Yes.

Jessie: That's weird, because it's usually the other way around. I've definitely felt in the middle of in-group/out-group situations at times. For those on the outside, the cleanup doesn't seem so bad. But from inside it is devastating. It weighs on your soul, it saturates you, you're tired and dragging, and you just want to sit in the middle of the chaos. You think, "There's no way I can even start picking this up."

Barb: I can relate to the shame as well as the exhaustion.

Jessie: Yes. But something happened about a year and a half ago that changed how I see this. I was student teaching at the university in the summer. They were constructing this new building on campus. I was teaching in the evening. When I left class the sun was setting behind the building. I was able to see the progress of constructing that building. Suddenly it hit me, that for the past four years I have been trying to find usable pieces among the devastation in my life. Here's a brick, and here's a door frame that might still work.

I felt as if I was rummaging through and finding things that would work, so I could start building up my little humble building again. All of a sudden I had this thought: the building I was building was almost identical to the one that had fallen when I got the diagnosis. What gets you is the diagnosis! People can be okay living with the illness until they get a diagnosis. Because that label is what really throws you!

Barb: Yes. It's like a word stuck on your forehead.

Jessie: Yes, it sticks, and I have mixed feelings about that. I didn't want to be like that first building, because that first building was flawed. But then I looked at my new building, which is coming out nicely, and it's coming out almost exactly like the first. I concluded that *I am not flawed*, that the bipolar disorder in my life is part of my design. It can be a tool, like my being personable, loud when I'm asking for help and fierce when I'm advocating for others. It's part of who I am, not a flaw.

That first "aha" moment in my adult life was when my husband accepted me. The second was realizing that my design elements are tools, not flaws. A third one is something I always talk about when I talk about my recovery. I was student teaching in a class on psychopathology. My teacher allowed me to lecture on mood disorders, affective disorders. So I lectured about all these things to a room of seventy five people. When I was done I thought, "Omigosh, I just talked about bipolar disorder without talking about me! That means that we're not one and the same." When bipolar disorder is a separate entity from me, we can discuss it and it doesn't have to be who I am.

TSUNAMI OF THE MIND

JOURNAL

I have a journal dedicated to my disorder. It's like any other relationship. It comes to bed with me and my husband, it helps me raise my kids, and it's there when I'm getting my coffee in the morning. I have a lifelong relationship with this thing. Sometimes when I'm a little hypomanic and also feeling okay I think, "Okay, we're getting along." Other times I think, "Mm, I don't really like you right now and I have three choice words for you."

For me recovery is having cycles that are manageable, like a quick up, a quick down, and also cycles that are more confined and further and further apart. Sometimes when you're hypomanic or manic, you look at the person in front of you and you go, "Really? Why in God's name would you want me *not* to be this way, 'cause I'm feeling pretty good right now!"

Barb: I can imagine that.

Jessie: That's one reason it's so hard to be compliant about medications. At that point you're so tired of being depressed that you just want to feel better. But that's the very time you need to take your meds so you won't flap all over the place.

I've had people tell me, "You're not sick enough." Some people are what I'd call very hard-core, saying, "This is the box you belong in, and these are all the drugs you should take, and it's a forever thing." On the other side you have all these fluffy bunny folks, saying, "Smile, pray hard, hope hard, and it will all be OK." That can be really irritating too.

Barb: I agree.

Jessie: But it helps me if I can meet in the middle and say, "OK, I have this physical condition, a *natural* condition." I need to lead my life with hope, being person-centered, always trying to have a positive attitude towards it, and taking the good from both sides. I need my medication. I know that there are people who say they function rather well without it. That's wonderful, but not all of us are that way.

Barb: Exactly.

Jessie: I'm neither advocating nor the opposite, but for me, I can't be well without medicine. But it needs to be a very holistic approach. That's where we're falling short. You can go to what I call these *"kumbaya"* meetings, with people who are all about the idea of just making a decision, just getting over it.

And then there are other places, those that have really big huge names for our problems. So I think that's the hard part. I just got a job, and because I'm a certified peer counselor, they said, "So what's something that you can bring to this new role?" I said, "Well, if a client brings with them a formal diagnosis from a doctor, with all these gigantic words that are enough to scare anybody - you can't pronounce them, you need all 4 years of education just to spell one – I can take that document and use my knowledge to support the person. The paper can be a starting point, but a person's life doesn't have to be contained by that diagnosis. We can define recovery and success together."

I'm in a loving marriage, my husband gives me butterflies after thirteen years, my kids are beautiful, I have my mother and my grandmother who love me and support me. My son gave a speech in May when I walked the stage at graduation. He said – and nobody told him to do this -- "I am proud of my mom. She took a class called 'stats.' I don't know what it is, but it made her cry. And she has to take a lot of medication, but I'm so happy that she's the best mom ever." I thought to myself, "Wow. That was it."

I'm blessed to have my support group. I'm blessed to be surrounded by people who love me and understand me unconditionally. And I'm involved in research. So now, even if things are difficult in practical ways like the economy being bad, I think that I'm more than "functional." That is something I want to stress. Sometimes a person says, "I just want to be functional." Don't have that "I just. . . ." attitude, because you can do so much more!

Barb: It's clear, Jessie, that you are much more than "functional."

Jessie: I think we all are. This condition is just something to live with. We live with beautiful oceans, with beautiful earth under our feet, with warmth from our sun, all of these things. Can they be destructive forces? Absolutely! Do we stop loving or needing them any less? No. The natural elements are sometimes good to us and sometimes not. We don't always know why, though we can speculate. Once in a while the tectonic plates just clash.

Barb: But none of us sent them a memo saying, "It's today!"

Jessie: Right. We may know that a thing happens and how it happens, but nobody can say exactly what made this thing happen at this moment. Thunderstorms and all these natural disasters are elements that we already live with. For people like us they are just a little more, ah –

Barb: Intense?

Jessie: Yes, intense, and a lot more touchy and volatile. It means we've got to watch the fire, the water, the earth [laughs], the air, all those things.

LANGUAGE

It helps if we take a holistic approach and say, for example, "I am a person living with a bipolar disorder." I had a talk with somebody who was involved in my senior thesis and was using the term "mentally ill." I had to speak up and say "No" to that phrase. The language that we wanted to use was person-first language, e.g. "living with a mental illness" as opposed to "mentally ill."

Barb: We have to keep saying it, because it's not always understood.

Jessie: The language is important, and it starts with me. I find myself correcting myself as well as correcting people around me. "I am a person who lives with bipolar disorder. I am not a bipolar person." That's where I think it starts, but it goes beyond the labels.

Barb. You talked about being compliant. I struggle with that word, because "compliant" is based on someone else's rules. It seems like a teacher speaking with a child. At the same time, I would like to see more people taking their medications consistently instead of saying to themselves, "I feel fine so I don't need any help anymore."

Part of the reason people may think they don't need anything more is that they don't understand these are natural phenomena, as you said earlier. Without that understanding, you can feel good and say, "Oh good, I'm going to be _well_ now." Because well versus ill is another dichotomy, like us versus them.

Jessie. Yes.

Barb: So which are we, Jessie? It seems to me we're both well and having a problem, healthy and living with an illness. There aren't a lot of places in life where both things can be true. But I think it's true in this case.

Jessie: This is where things like your faith come in. It's going to be different for everybody: how we treat it, what we believe about it, the influence it has over us, the influence we have over it – all those things. For me, compliance means that I need to stick to my treatment. I need to stick to exercise, to having a positive attitude. If I don't comply with the standards that I have set for myself and my own recovery, certain things are not going to get done. But yes, there is that dichotomy.

I am well, in terms of having a good life. My daughter has autism; she sees the world in a very different way from the way I do. But she's got this amazing sense of humor and she's bright and she's smart. We all have something going on. It's like a continuum, and sometimes we're more on this side.

My mentor said in class, "I'm obligated to teach you about the DSM (Diagnostic and Statistical Manual of Mental Disorders) and its categories. But I want you guys to know that those statistics simply mean that somebody somewhere decided it took five or six symptoms to meet the criteria for X disorder. What if you meet four of them? Do you not get help?" We have to think about these things holistically and know that they manifest differently in everybody.

THE ENVELOPES

You have to understand yourself. I can't overstress the importance of that. When I start "going up," I notice the color red everywhere. When I see that's happening I say to myself, "Okay, it's time to go to my Up Envelope." I have three big yellow envelopes marked Down, Up, and

Mixed. I have recorded an audio CD for myself in each envelope. I put together the three envelopes because I decided that no one can be more reliable, or more likely for me to believe, than me.

When I plop in the Up CD, my voice says, "Hi, Jessie. If you're talking to me right now it's because you're on your way up. Turn in your keys, credit cards, phone, computer, your meds, and any alcohol in your house to your husband. Do that now. Pause me, and I'll be here, waiting." I get all these things together and give them to my husband. Then I come back to the tape and I hear, "OK." I get six hours to be with my mania and enjoy it. The Up envelope includes two music box mechanisms that I can tinker with if I want, or I can do whatever keeps me busy for six hours. At the end of that time I can pout, cry, or have a tantrum. Then I take my meds.

The Down envelope CD has a longer speech. When I am going down, my voice says, "No, you're not worthless; you're not a burden; it's okay." I have to literally hear myself say it on this tape, because I can't say it to myself in person yet. I have a gift card or something in there that's special, only to be used if I have to open this folder. The Mixed envelope is tricky, because there's a lot of confusion, a lot of turbulence going on.

Coping skills for everybody are going to be different. You have to learn about yourself, be aware, get in touch with others who are going through the same thing, educate yourself, and *advocate* for yourself. Don't let somebody just push medicine down your throat, or ignore the full person you are. That's important even in a situation like mine when I don't have a psychiatrist, and have a psychiatric nurse practitioner.

Barb: I also have a psychiatric mental health nurse practitioner who is a good listener.

NATURE AND HOPE

Jessie: The reason I decided to come to talk to you is that I've had trouble lately seeing past my disorder and toward furthering my education and publishing my studies. When we first talked on the phone I saw you as an educated woman who is advocating for others through telling their stories. I wanted to connect with that hope. The more we connect, the stronger we can be.

Barb: You're right. A major reason I've wanted to have these conversations is to advocate for better understanding. What else do you want to say about that?

Jessie: Many professionals don't seem to realize that if someone is hypomanic, they do not want to be taken out of a positive state. If you have bipolar depression and spend a lot of time down in the dumps, when you start to feel better you're going to want to enjoy it, whatever the therapist says. And some professionals don't understand what it's like to be in a mixed episode, where you don't know which way is up, so the therapists may have to repeat themselves. These are human experiences!

Some professionals act as if their job is to treat your symptoms, believing that there's no cure for the mood. At times it seems as if the providers think that your body isn't hurting, so that's all that matters.

Barb: That's a problem. Many doctors don't know how harrowing the inner pain can be. They don't believe that you can feel like you're going to die. Someone I knew who had never gotten sick in his whole life got the flu. He said to me, "This is the end of my life." For this person the flu felt ultimate. I thought to myself, "If the flu can feel like the end of things, so can a tsunami of the mind." But as my dear grandfather said when I was a child, "The good book says, it came to pass; it doesn't say it came to stay." Experiences do not last forever.

I'm grateful that you and I have had a chance to meet and talk today about things that are important to us both. I wouldn't have chosen to be suicidal when I was a doctoral student, but many years later I have a chance to be here with you now. Our conversation opens a door between us. We both want to make a difference for other people, and we can.

Jessie: That's what I wanted to tell you, when I had the epiphany about the two buildings. It's that the second building looks a lot like the first one. This is my design, this is natural, and this is who I was meant to be.

If we had a choice we wouldn't want to get to the point of being suicidal, or become overweight because of the medications. But you see people from Winston Churchill to Thomas Gray to all these other people who have touched on something. It may have been either very bright or very dark, but there was no way they could have accessed that without surfing on top of this tsunami wave or getting thrown to the bottom of it. There's something about it that can be a gift, as Kay Jamieson writes in her book *Touched with Fire*.[11]

There are moments that I get along with my disorder all right. I'm well today, thank you, I had some creativity to finish the essay I was working on, and it makes me who I am. It makes me accessible to others, and I get to meet people who speak my language. When I see one person nod when I'm telling my story in front of people, I know I'm saying something that person can hear but can't yet say.

Barb: People can hear it in their hearts.

Jessie: After I have done a talk, I go home and write down what I've said, so I will remember what connected with another person. Being in the place I am now makes me strong, makes me unique, and enhances so many of my gifts. And it propels me. I don't think it's all bad to have a disorder. It's uncomfortable as heck, but it's not necessarily a death sentence. You just have to have the right tools to get through it, the right people, and the right listeners. This is why it's so important to have mental health professionals and primary care doctors become educated.

COMMUNITY

We're working with the Spokane police force to help them understand better the people they're dealing with. Call them patients, clients, or consumers, these people are not "crazies," but people with an illness like epilepsy that can lead to an attack or a seizure.

Barb: Right. And a person in diabetic shock or having a stroke can appear to strangers as being drunk.

Jessie: Exactly. In the study that we did about community perceptions of mental illness, either a Latino man or a white man had committed involuntary manslaughter, criminal negligence. The research participants were 150 people from all over Spokane. They were told that either man could have been on medication and crashed. Our results showed a positive significance, with many more people saying the man needed a less harsh sentence because of a mental illness, and needed treatment. They agreed that throwing the man in prison was not going to help anybody.

That tells me that programs like NAMI, diversity talks, and other organizations are touching people, little by little. And I've been able to connect with a lot of people, in my classes and research and family and community. I'm an investment.

Barb: Yes. And the return on investment – ROI –comes in many directions. For me, the return on investment is that after hearing these stories I will make them available to other people. Then *Tsunami of the Mind* will be read by someone who says, "Oh, I get it," and tells that to somebody else who says, "Oh, I get it," a ripple effect. However big or small the ripples are, this is what I am called to do at this point in my life.

Jessie: Now that we've met and talked, I can see what you are trying to do and why. The interviews and stories can be healing for the people who hear them as well as for you. Hopefully we will reduce the stigma about these things.

Barb: I hope for that too. Thank you, Jessie, for being willing to talk with me. We are no longer strangers!

MIKE

My wife Janie is very patient. She took a lot of crap that she shouldn't have had to put up with. Most women would have said "Screw you!" and left me, and rightfully so. She saw the good side of me and wanted to do what she could to draw that out. It worked out. — Mike

I MET MIKE through a family friend who worked with him on house re-modeling projects. Mike was interested in talking with me because he wanted to stay well despite back surgery and changes in medications. We met first in December 2012, in August 2014, and by phone in 2015.

Barb: Mike, our mutual friend told me that you had a lot of hard things happen in your life, and you've managed to get through them. I'm interested in what I call tsunamis of the mind – what they feel like on the inside and what it's like to survive them and go forward. I'm grateful that you wanted to talk with me.

I've found from my own life and from other people that what goes on early in your life has an impact on what happens later. What was your family like when you were growing up?

EARLY YEARS

Mike: I had a really good childhood. My dad, actually my stepfather Raymond, married my mother when I was quite young. My mother had married for the first time when she was 15. My older brother was born when she was 16, and I was born when she was 17½ years old.

What I heard about my original father was that he was lazy and didn't do anything to support the family. Mom worked hard as a waitress. She divorced him when I was about 2 years old, and she married Raymond when I was 3½ or 4 years old. I always went by his last name, though my adoption wasn't final till I was in the eighth grade. When I met my original dad after getting out of the Army, he wasn't somebody that I wanted to call Dad [laughs].

Barb: How many children were there in all?

Mike: There were four of us: my older brother and me, and a half brother and sister from my mother's marriage to Raymond. Raymond always treated us well. There was never any abuse. When I got spankings with a belt, I deserved them. The spankings did a lot to keep me under control.

Fortunately I was allowed to play sports. I played football, baseball and basketball, and I was all city quarterback in Seattle. I often stayed at the gym till nine o'clock at night, and I'd get up at six a.m., especially in warmer weather. I'd practice pitching a hard ball against the brick wall at the side of our house. Some of the neighbors didn't like the noise from that!

I did well in school until high school, and then I got kind of flakey. I think that's when the manic depression started, though it was not diagnosed then. I knew everybody in high school, and I had a pretty good time. I was hell-bent to learn to smoke.

Barb: And you learned! [Mike takes a smoke break during the interview.] What else did you do in high school that you'd call flakey?

Mike: I ran away from home a couple of times for a day or two. I was ornery, sassy, and a hard kid to raise. I wanted to do my own thing, and to do whatever came to mind.

But I was also a good worker. I started working before I was 12 and through high school. I delivered the weekly *Ballard Tribune* to 360 customers, then the *Seattle Times* until I was 16. Then I was hired as a solicitor. I knocked on doors where the paperboy knew the people weren't yet getting the *Seattle Times*. I was successful with that, and it was decent money, so I could go on dates and buy things my parents couldn't cover. I also worked for a professional gardener in high school.

We were a hardworking family. We kids always had our chores, and we didn't get an allowance. When I was in third grade we spent our weekends and vacations remodeling houses. Both my parents worked hard. Later, after having four children, my mother went back and got a master's degree in education. She was teaching in Seattle until she passed away.

Dad was an engineer working for the Army Corps of Engineers. Two months before the end of my senior year he was sent to Japan, and he was second in command there. My older brother was already in the army, and he transferred to Korea when I went into the army myself. My dad had to retire medically because of Hodgkin's Disease. He died at the age of 58. That was a rough time for all of us.

THE ARMY

Barb: How old were you when you went into the army?

Mike: I went in August 5th 1967, just before my 18th birthday. There were some incidents in the army that I can trace back to the beginning of a diagnosis of bipolar. The first incident was my going AWOL when I was almost finished with a training school to become a helicopter mechanic. I would have graduated third in my class, but I never graduated from the school because of the AWOL.

Barb: Were you bored at the training school?

Mike: Extremely. I was active in sports, and we had a gym that was only two blocks from my company area. I was frequently there when we weren't on duty or going to school. I found mechanic school more like high school, with lectures so boring that I could go to sleep standing up in the classroom [laughs]. And with all that I was still one of the top students there.

Barb: You knew you were smart, but you didn't like being in school.

Mike: Right. Things just wouldn't happen fast enough for me. I'd get bored, really hyper, and I'd go into a manic phase. I'd go and go until I had no energy left. Then I'd have the problem of not thinking clearly and not considering the consequences of my actions.

Barb: What was your sleep like when you were wound up, or when it was warmer weather? I've read that during spring and summer people can have a hard time getting enough sleep.

Mike: When I was in the army I could go for two weeks on two to three hours of sleep. Until recently five hours has been more than enough sleep. Now I typically go to bed at 8 o'clock and I'm asleep until three or four a.m. That's the most sleep I've had since I was a very young kid.

I went AWOL (absent without leave) for 29 days while on a manic high. I hitchhiked down to Florida and purchased a 25 caliber Beretta pistol on the way. But when we ran out of gas on the way to Florida I had to sell the gun.

In Florida I was picking oranges on the graveyard shift. I became suicidal one night and took a large number of Contac capsules. Then I turned myself in to the Florida State Patrol. They got me in touch with my base up north and had me sent back to Fort Walker. There was a special court martial and I was demoted to orderly.

[Mike told me later by phone that he learned about this first suicide attempt from Army records that were part of his application for disability benefits. He had not remembered that event earlier. It happened prior to his getting married.]

Another time in the Army I spent 76 days in the Fort Benning Stockade for misappropriating an automobile while I was on a manic high. The car owner was in the hospital. I blew his engine, but I paid for the car to be rebuilt with a new engine, so the guy saw no reason to press charges. When I transferred companies, the new commanding officer decided to press charges.

I got six months in jail and reduction of pay to E-1, as low a private as you can get. After all those days in the stockade I was thinking more clearly. So I asked to see the commander of the stockade, and I told him I realized the importance of completing my service with an honorable discharge. Two days after our talk he arranged for me to go back to regular duty.

Then I was sent to Vietnam. When I was near the point of getting out of there and going home, I got really drunk. I nearly stood another court-martial, and that would have wiped out everything. I got out of that one by some fast talking, so I completed my army career in just shy of three years.

MARRIAGE

I met Janie before I went to Vietnam. We knew of each other for just a week. We went out once, and we eloped that afternoon. That was 1969. We've been married now for 45 years!

Barb: Wow. I would call that lucky!

Mike: I'm most fortunate. I couldn't be where I'm at today without her. Janie is very patient. She took a lot of crap that she shouldn't have had to put up with. Most women would have said "Screw you!" and left me - - and rightfully so. She saw the good side of me and wanted to do what she could to draw that out. It's worked out.

We started our own business in 1981. Through her diligence, and hard work by both of us, we managed to keep things under control despite some episodes of mine that gave us problems. Janie has a great business sense for keeping things going. Eventually I turned over all the finances to her so that I didn't have any ready money for me to go wild with.

The remodeling service we did provided me with enough physical activity to keep me from going off the deep end most of the time. Now she is running it all by herself while I'm getting over my back surgery and sitting in this chair. Bless her heart! She works so hard for us.

I took several different medications over the years, starting with lithium, then Depakote. Those two just made me like a zombie. I would just manage to get to work every day and do what I had to do.

[Asks Janie]: How long have I been on the risperidone?

Janie: Two years in August.

Mike: That medicine has been a godsend. It really keeps me on an even keel. I am using the risperidone along with medical marijuana, which is primarily for pain control but also helps me keep a positive attitude.

Barb: I think you said your first back surgery was five weeks ago. That's not a long time ago.

Mike: I know. By and large I'm happy with the way the surgery has gone. I can walk to the end of the block and back now, and not feel like I'm going to collapse. Before the surgery I was hard-pressed even to make it to the end of the driveway. It's all a healing process. You're familiar with that, I guess.

Barb: Right. [Barbara had low back surgery in 2011 and was working in her backyard prior to this conversation.]

Mike: Once I get through the healing, I expect things to get somewhat back to normal. Walking is relatively easy. I don't have the strength yet, but it will come as the pain dissipates. I'm encouraged by your experience. If you can dig out blackberry roots, you're in good shape!

Both laugh.

CYCLES

Mike: I'm very cyclic. I remember in high school especially, I had a lot of energy in the warmer months. Then after that the highs and lows started happening. Those have been around for a lot of years. I haven't had the cycles so much since I've been taking the risperidone.

I trace a lot of the things I did earlier in my life to the cycles. When I first started learning about bipolar or manic depression, those things started to make more sense.

A psychiatrist diagnosed me as a psychotic manic depressive because I had attempted suicide. I attempted suicide three or four times. I don't remember the details, but I know the doctor told Janie on one of those occasions that I wouldn't make it through the night.

Barb: You said that you took pills each time. You didn't have a gun nearby?

Mike: Early on I had a rifle, but it never occurred to me to use it. After I had a suicide attempt, I did sell my rifle. Selling it caused a few problems in the family, since it was a hand-me-down from my dad. I loved that rifle. I learned to shoot when I was 11 years old and started hunting with my dad. When I turned 12 and took a gun safety course, I was able to get my hunting license. I killed my first deer when I was home on leave, just before I went to Vietnam. In all I think I've killed three deer in my life. [He laughs]

I got out of the army September 5, and September 23d was my 21st birthday. Then alcohol became a problem, and that contributed greatly to the depression. Anything that goes up must come down. I'd have those super highs - - way up here! - - and then whump, I'm in these deep dark depressions. Nothing made me happy. I was angry about everything, and quite belligerent.

Barb: Did you get in a lot of fights?

Mike: I could have. I had a big mouth back then, but somehow I talked my way out of a lot of fights. I would get drunk in a tavern, and somebody would say something and we'd mince words and there we'd go. I learned a lot of self-defense in the army, and I needed it. I was 6'1" and weighed only 127 pounds, but what I had was all muscle.

I was no match for big people like my older brother. He is 6'3" and 235 pounds. He and I once got in a fight when he was home on leave. We were doing that old hand-slap thing. When I was beating him at that, he just reached over and took me by the back of my shirt, threw me over his head, and put me over the top of our eight foot fence in the backyard. [laughs].

Barb: He could do that?

Mike: Yes, he was that strong. So that ended the fight. We had a lot of fights over the years. I don't know if it had anything to do with my bipolar issues. I think somewhere along the line I stopped competing with him. Once I stopped competing with him we got along.

Did you know that Robin Williams passed away yesterday? He killed himself.[12]

Barb: [Gasps] No!

Mike: Nobody said anything about him having bipolar, but I believe he had it, whether or not he had been diagnosed. He clearly did suffer.

Barb: And he had that high energy. You can't be much more energetic than he was!

Mike: I read that he had been deeply depressed over the last month or so. His closest friends and his wife recognized it, but he didn't admit himself to a hospital for additional care this time.

Barb: What a terrible loss!

Mike: Yes. He's the same age as Janie, 63 years old.

I'm so grateful that I haven't had any of the depression now that I am taking the risperidone medicine. It seems to be working. I've had a little bit of the high, but not *high,* not skyrocketing.

Barb: So you haven't felt out of control.

Mike: Exactly. It's been difficult with the surgery, not being able to get up and move and do the work.

Barb: I can see how hard that would be for you. You started working on a paper route before you were 12 years old, and you've kept going ever since!

GOING AWAY

Mike: I've never been without a job, even when I left home and Janie and the kids. I went down to Redding, California, for three months, and in 24 hours I had a job down there. I kind of forced my way in at a construction site.

Barb: You went down there under what circumstances?

Mike: I just left. I had done a job out in Ridgefield and got paid $2400 in cash. That was my first manic blackout. I drove from Ridgefield to a place on the highway, pulled off at a corner, and couldn't figure out how I got there. So I thought," I've got to have a drink." I went into the nearest tavern and got drunk. Then I thought, "Screw this. I'm out of here." I had the clothes on my back and my tools and stuff in my truck. I didn't go home; I just left. I picked up a couple of hitchhikers, drove down to Redding, found a place to stay, and got a job. The guy offered me a 60-40 percent cut in his business, a full-fledged contract.   [He pauses.]

The weekends were what got me. There was not a lot to do except go to the tavern. I got tired of doing that, so I'd go to the mall and try to meet a young lady. But at the mall I'd see all these kids who were my kids' ages, and I missed my family dearly. Finally one day I called Janie and begged her to let me come back. And she said, "Yeah, you can come home. I want you home." So I came back home.

Barb: It sounds like your trip to California was impulsive, rather than a decision to leave Janie or the family.

Mike: Very much so. I just went. And I made the most of that for the first month or so. Then I came down from the high and really started to miss my family. It took a while to build up the courage to call Janie. She didn't hear from me for two months, and she had no idea if I was dead or alive. The $2400 had been supposed to pay the bills. I'm still not sure how she managed to pull it all together, bless her heart.

Barb: How old were the kids at that time?

Mike: I'm 20 years older than my son, so they would have been 4 and 5 or 4 and 6 years old. At the time of my last suicide attempt they were already out of the house. That last time was an aspirin overdose.

Barb: Do you remember what was happening at that time?

Mike: I think I went way too long without any medications, four or five years. As I recall they were relatively good years. There were no major problems until that suicide attempt.

Barb: Do you recall taking medications during those years?

Mike: I think I took only Depakote at that time. I don't remember what triggered the depression. It might have been one of those times when I had done something off the wall or just not right. Again I decided that the world would be better off - and Janie - without me.

I kept thinking that if I was out of the picture, Janie would find some-body really decent. I was going into this deep dark hole, and I got drunk on top of it. I took a full bottle of aspirin I'd gotten at the Safeway store across the street. I know there were 78 aspirin. There was a count on the bottle and I took all of them.

They didn't expect me to survive that. I was at the Trauma Center, vomiting blood. But somehow I survived it. After that attempt I got on a different medication and stayed on that one for quite a while. But when I started going through all this back pain, they took me off of all my medications to get me onto the pain medication.

Barb: Again you were very lucky! I know that the illnesses referred to as bipolar are complicated, and they are hard for doctors to diagnose and treat effectively. You and I have had different histories. I experi-enced depression during high school, and your first vivid experiences were more the manic ones.

Mike: Yes, I'd get very, very high. I could just go for hours. Nobody could keep up with me. Workwise, that was a good thing. I could do twice as much work as all of my help combined. I just never stopped. When I was painting up high, I started with my left hand and then switched to the other hand and used both.

THE LEFT HAND

Barb: Did you write with your left hand when you were growing up?

Mike: I'm left-handed but almost entirely ambidextrous. I can write legibly with my right hand, but slowly. Typically I do the finer things left-handed. When I'm eating a steak, I have no trouble feeding myself with my left hand. And if I'm picking up a forkful of peas, I want to do that left-handed!

Barb: Did anyone try to stop you from being left-handed?

Mike: Actually they did at school, but my mother threw a fit. Sometime between third and sixth grade they decided kids should be right-handed. So I started getting chastised, and I came home crying to my mother. She went to school and said to them, "He's left-handed, and you're not going to change him, so don't even try." So that ended that.

You are what you are. If you're left-handed, you're left-handed, so you learn to live with it. But in school I threw a baseball right-handed and a football right-handed. I served tennis left-handed, but if I had an overhand smash coming on the right side I had no problem switching hands and driving the ball home.

It was almost unfair to play tennis against me. I had a backhand but didn't have to depend on it. I could do the forehand with either side, and I had quick enough reflexes to be able to switch hands whenever I wanted.

Barb: Have you played tennis in recent years?

Mike: Not in the past five or ten years. I haven't been well enough, and my back has been too big of an issue. I may play again, but the hardest thing in tennis is the pounding you take on the court. I'll be happy if I can walk. We like to hike the trails, go up in the woods, and do a lot of camping. I've even hunted with bow and arrow. That was a lot of fun, though I've never hit one.

SOCCER

One of the best things I ever did was to teach my kids soccer. I did that for five years and was quite successful. We wound up taking second place in the state, two years in a row.

Barb: What age group were they?

Mike: I started the eight girls when they were just under 8 years old. I coached them until they were 14 and later with indoor soccer in Portland. They fired me as their coach at that point. They were at the age when they thought they could handle it on their own.

Barb: The girls fired *you?*

Mike: Yes. They decided they didn't need a coach anymore. Interestingly, we had never lost a game up until then, and after that they never won a game. [Both laugh]

Barb: Have you reminded them of this?

Mike: I never had to. When I run into any of the kids, they say, "We screwed up. We should never have fired you!" [laughs] But every kid who was on my soccer team finished college. I always encouraged education, even though I had less than a year and a half of college myself. I told them, "If you don't get the good grades, you can't play. So make up your mind." So they all came through. I get posts on Facebook all the time from kids who were on the team. And my son stays in touch with everybody. He's far more socialized than I am.

FAMILY

Barb: Where does your son live?

Mike: He's in the Sacramento area, a little east of Sacramento.

Barb: What is his family situation?

Mike: He's divorced and remarried. He had two kids of his own, and his second wife has two kids, and they don't plan on having any more kids. He's 45 and currently has his own computer business. He is quite good with motivating people.

Barb: Where is your daughter?

Mike: She lives here in Vancouver, 10 minutes away from us. She's got a really good job with a firm based in Nashville. She goes to Nashville a week out of every month. She heads up the staff that puts together promotional materials and advertising for KinderCare. It's a lot of responsibility.

Barb: They sound as if the apple hasn't fallen far from the tree! You talked about Janie holding the business together for many years, and you've been working since you were 12 years old.

Mike: Our kids learned to work early too. They were 11 or 12 when they started helping us on the weekends, even if it was nothing more than cleaning up the sheetrock mess in the house. Both of them had a paper route before I started my business, so they've always earned their own way.

Barb: Has either of them talked with you about having mood cycles or depression?

Mike: My daughter has talked a little with me about depression, and she gets a little hyperactive at times. But she's never left home or shirked her responsibilities. She talks more about it with Janie than with me. I don't know if she's on any medication at this point. But she and I have had some deep discussions about what she remembers of my manic and depressive states. Neither of my children has been diagnosed, and so far none of the grandchildren has been diagnosed. We have four of our own, and four adopted ones by my son and my daughter. We went from four grandchildren to eight within a year and a half!

Barb: That's quite a family! Mike, you've referred to the terms bipolar disorder and manic depression during our talk. Do you recall when you were given the diagnosis of manic depression?

DIAGNOSIS

Mike: Yes. One time after I had made a suicide attempt, I was released from the hospital and into what was then Columbia Humana, a mental health care facility a few blocks from here. I was still groggy from all the medications I'd had in the hospital. My first night at the facility, the psychiatrist walked into his office, asked me to take a seat, and said, "Sir, you are a psychotic manic depressive. The cure rate for psychotic manic depressives is less than one percent. However, we can control it with certain medications."

Barb: Did he actually *say* the cure rate is one percent?

Mike: Yes. "The cure rate for psychotic manic depressives is *less* than one percent." They have no real known cure. After I had been told I had manic depression- -they didn't call it bipolar then - -I spent a month at Dammasch State Hospital in Oregon, where they were trying to figure out what was going on with me. But I knew I was there at the wrong time. I had just come off of a major depressive episode, so they didn't learn anything new. In the month I spent there, I I was mainly cheap help for the hospital!

Barb: What did you do while you were there?

Mike: I helped the caregivers. I worked with the kids in the gym, played a lot of basketball, and taught people about my trade as a handyman. A handyman can legitimately go through a house from the ground up, including the wiring, plumbing, and roofing. So at Dammasch Hospital I had a chance to teach people what I know. That's what I am doing now with the young man who is living here with us. He's a good carpenter in his own right. He also has bipolar. I knew that when I hired him.

Barb: Had he told you?

Mike: After watching him and seeing how he acted, I asked him what kind of problems he had, and he said he had bipolar. I asked him, "Are you medicated?" He did have medication when I hired him, but right now he doesn't have insurance. He's maintaining really well, though, and he works well with Janie. She can give him his assignment and he knows he has to stay on top of a job. If he's not on track he can get really forgetful and drop the ball.

Barb: So in a sense you're his family.

Mike: That's pretty much it. At this stage in his life we're the best thing that could happen to him. He has a place to live, pays rent, and Janie controls the paycheck just like she does with me. He and I are both not very good with handling money! In my case my allowance is $20 a week when we have money coming in.

Barb: What do you do with your allowance?

CARVING

Mike: I purchase these carving knives and the wood for making chess pieces. Here are four of the pieces I've made so far: the castle, the king, the bishop, and the knight. Thirty-two pieces make up a full set.

Barb: When did you start the chess pieces - - before or after your back surgery?

Mike: I started playing with the wood back in November, before the surgery. I don't spend all my time on this. I have to be in the right mood for it. I look at different designs and then try to work with the grain of the wood.

Barb: That looks like a big task, carving a whole set of chess pieces!

Mike: For sure. Several of my grandchildren play chess. I had the idea of making a hand-carved chess set as a keepsake from Grandpa. They're fun to do, but I'm a real amateur. I got a lot of the ideas online. I'm using bass wood, which is hard to harvest but easy to carve.

It's quite an experience figuring out what you're going to take away. The highest points here are the original block. Everything else has to be chiseled away. You have to envision it ahead of time, then figure out what cuts to make. It's creating negative space. You take away part of the wood to create the design you want.

I've got some modeling clay downstairs that I can also play with. I made a horse in clay so I'd have an image and know what needed to be taken away. With clay you can screw it up, then get it warm and redo it, but once you cut a piece of wood away it's gone! [laughs]

Barb: Wasn't it Michelangelo who wrote about working with a large slab of marble and finding David inside it?

Mike: That's how it goes in working with this wood. Each piece is different. The grain of the wood won't always let you cut exactly what you think you're going to cut. So it's quite the learning experience. It keeps my mind occupied. I think that's an important part of aging, to stay mentally active.

The grandchildren got excited when they heard I was going to do this. My dad was a chess buff and played in state tournaments, and we kids played a lot of chess. There were no video games then!

Barb: Did you do any woodcarving when you were growing up?

Mike: No. I worked with wood in construction, but that's a whole different ball game. You don't have the detail except in finish work. One idea I got is to use both sides of the block. Here's the queen, and the king. I haven't finished her eyes and eyebrows yet. I'm learning to do eyes.

Barb: I'm told that in many kinds of art the eyes are the hardest part.

Mike: Now I want to show you something else. [He goes into another room.] All of these pictures are Janie's artwork. I'd like to have a showing of her paintings sometime. She is fabulous with it!

Barb: You talked earlier about being left-handed. As you may know, the brain's right hemisphere is the one stronger in art and music, in imagination and seeing the big picture. It seems like you are someone who sees both the big picture and the details. That's quite a gift! As we finish, is there anything else you want to tell me?

Mike: Yes. It was a real battle coming out of depression. I had to learn to take every little success as a plus, and to build on those stepping stones to work my way back to feeling like I had a place in society. I needed those successes in coaching soccer, the successes we have had with the business, and the number of clientele we still have today from our earliest clients. We earned the right to have them continue to work with us.

Barb: In all of those instances, respect and trust are important.

Mike: Exactly. That's always been a big thing for us. Without the trust you're going nowhere. You have to earn that. That was the way I was raised. My dad said, "Dammit, if it's worth doing, do it right." [laughs]

Barb: I can relate to that. When I've had a hard time – whether from depression or anxiety – I'd worry that I might lose someone's trust and be unable to do something I cared about. It must have been hard for Janie when she had to keep the business going when you weren't around.

Mike: Definitely. When I was gone for months at a time, Janie kept things going until I got back. It would be at the end of a major job, so the clientele didn't have to get mad at me. I've been very fortunate in that. Janie never had to whip me to go to work. I *wanted* to go to work, and I loved what I did. We were making people's dreams come true. And in our own house we've done the hardwood floors, tiles, kitchen cabinets, and all the detail around the doors.

Barb: It's clear that you both love doing this work.

Mike: Particularly for bipolar people, the more time you have to do nothing, the worse off you are. You have to find a way to stay active, to keep your mind going. For me it's been a real struggle with the back surgery, and not being able to get up and move. But I'm starting to walk now, first to the mailbox, then down the street.

Barb: Having had back surgery myself, I know it takes time to heal. But it's great that you're doing something creative while you're healing. And you and Janie are also helping a young man develop his own skills and work ethic.

Thank you, Mike, for a great conversation!

LORI

I was able to share my story in a 12-step meeting. A woman there needed to know that I survived, that I got through it. I am so grateful. I'm getting to experience pain and difficulties in life too. I like to think of this image from when we were growing up, the little blow-up dolls. When you punch them, they jump right up. That's how I feel in my life. When you punch me in the butt I get up, because I use my tools. — Lori

---

LORI AND I met by phone in 2011, when I was volunteering for NAMI Washington. Lori was given my phone number and she called me at home. She felt close to suicide but was trying to find help in order to stay alive. We emailed and talked with each other during the following month. This phone conversation took place in 2013.

Barb: It's exciting for me to talk with you now. It's over two years since we first talked and emailed. Rereading our emails from that time was vivid, and frightening.

Lori: Was it frightening for you too?

Barb: Oh yes! There seemed to be huge waves overwhelming you while you were trying hard to stay alive. You were desperate, and you went first to a doctor, then to a hospital, and then you were told you had to go to another hospital in order to be seen.

Lori: That was awful. But I'm here now, thank God!

Barb: I agree. And I thank you for being on this call with me.

TRAUMA

Barb: Can we go back to what your early life was like? You had mentioned an early trauma. Was it sexual trauma?

Lori: Yes, partly. It started when I was about 4 years old. The abusers were two neighbor kids, twin sisters who were 12 or 13 years old. They must have had horrible abuse in their own lives to do the things they did to me. It was constant harassment, not just sexual trauma. One time they tied my hands to a swing, pulled my legs back, and let my body drag across the ground through the gravel. Once they lured me into a shed by telling me my baby sister was in there. They shoved me in and locked the door for what felt like hours. A bit later my older sister came by and they threw her in with me. We screamed bloody murder. Another time they took me and my older sister out in the woods, ran away, and left us there to find our way home in the dark.

I only remember one sexual trauma incident, although I might have blocked others out. I won't go into the specifics, except to say that objects were involved.

Barb: For how long did this harassment happen?

Lori: From age 4 until we moved away, just before I started kindergarten.

Barb: Were you able to tell anybody about it?

Lori: No. They threatened to kill my baby sister. And my mother was going through a deep depression herself. My dad was out drinking at night, and I think my mom was just going through the motions of taking care of my older sister and me. We got bathed and fed, and that was it. I know she loved us, but she wasn't there emotionally.

Part of what happened was not her fault. At 4 years old I didn't know how to tell her what the girls were doing to me. The day of the sexual trauma I ran home and didn't get to the bathroom in time. My mother didn't see the physical signs of what had happened, so I got spanked and told, "Naughty girl; clean up your mess." Years later I recognize that my mom did what she could that day. I won't waste one more second of my life blaming her.

PARENTS

Barb: You said your mother had depression and that your dad drank. How much of that did you observe when you were growing up?

Lori: My parents never allowed us to see anything negative in the household. My dad drank when he was out, so I didn't know he was an alcoholic until I was in my teens. At that point I began seeing him come home all beat up, not knowing where his car was, or with his car having run into a tree. He also was drunk in front of my friends.

Only once did I see him drunk before then. I was 12 years old, and it scared me to death. It was Christmas Day and we were at our relatives' house. There was a lot of hard liquor around. My dad had a smirk on his face and was chasing me all over the living room with a ladybug toy I'd been given. There was a strange look in his eye. I ran to my mom and said, "I don't want to play with Dad. He's scaring me." I had been the apple of his eye, but this time was different, and creepy.

Barb: It sounds as if you were being intuitive. What did your mom said to you that day?

Lori: She just asked me, "Why are you afraid?" I didn't have an answer. I just said, "I don't know, I'm just scared." So I went out in the backyard. We were living in California, so I just played outside. My dad was usually a beer drinker, but not that day. I'd never seen him act that way with me before. And I never saw my parents argue or give each other the silent treatment.

Barb: But it sounds like you knew some things were happening. How early in your life did you know your mother was depressed?

Lori: I didn't know that for sure until I was an adult and started to talk with her about it. When I was battling depression myself I realized she had acted the way I felt as an adult, with a look in her eye that she was someplace else. Once when I was a child she was sitting at the breakfast table in her bathrobe. She was leaning against the wall with her arms folded, very silent. I went up to her and I said, "Mommy, I love you," and I tried to reach my arms around her. She pushed me away and said, "Leave me alone. I don't love you anymore." I felt unloved at that point, but now I realize that she was hurting a great deal, angry not at me but at my dad. When he came home drunk at night, he had been sleeping with one of her friends. I didn't remember that early incident with my mother until I was an adult and the memories of my abuse started coming back. Fortunately that behavior never happened again.

Barb: You have an older and a younger sister. Have you stayed close with them?

Lori: Yes! They're my family best friends, even though we live far away from each other. My younger sister's in Texas and my older sister's still in California. We've all had mental health challenges. I had thought of us as the proverbial happy American family until we were adults and I started talking with my sisters about our childhood. Then I started to realize things that were not normal.

Barb: What kinds of things?

Lori: We girls didn't learn how to handle conflict. On the one hand, when my sisters and I would fight we'd get a spanking or a reprimand, so we knew not to be disrespectful to our parents. But one time one of my sisters sassed my mom, and my mom backed her up against the wall and started smacking her around the face until my sister had a bloody nose. That was scary!

CALIFORNIA MOVE

The year we moved from Washington to California was hard in many ways. We lived in Tacoma until I was 11. I was told that my dad had a company he wanted to work for, and my sisters thought it would be cool to live in California. I didn't hear about the move until after both of my sisters knew. My parents felt I was emotionally fragile but they didn't know anything about depression. They waited till later to tell me, so the move was more of a shock to me than to my sisters.

We left Washington at four in the morning, and we all cried for the first hundred miles. I'd never seen my dad cry. My mom had to keep handing him Kleenex. He was leaving the home he'd had all his life. One of us said, "Why are we all crying?" I don't remember anyone answering, but it was definitely hard for all of us.

We moved first to San Gabriel and then to a little town called Sierra Madre. I had my first real depression in California, though I didn't recognize it until later. During the first year I had to go to a new school where almost all the children were Latino. My sisters and

I were three of maybe 20 white people in the whole school. They made fun of us, so it was a really lonely time. My mom was acting kind of funny too.

By then I was 13, and I didn't know anybody very well. We rented a house that was near another little house with five kids. One of the kids was a girl who became a close friend for a while. She was rebellious, and I was afraid of her. She started getting into boys and pot and smoking. I didn't do the pot or the boy thing, but I started smoking with the girls. I was always scared.

Barb: What was it like at school?

Lori: Well, a wonderful thing happened at the start of junior high school. I met the school counselor, who was an amazing woman. She called me into her office and said, "I'm the counselor. I'd just like to get to know you. I like to know my students." I had all these feelings of anxiety and fear that year. One day I felt like my mind was in a fetal position. I couldn't speak. She took my hand, and we just sat there for the whole period. Then she said, "Lori, you're going to be okay." I will never forget that woman. She was a refuge for me, one of the most amazing women in my life. I hope I see her again in heaven.

Barb: In my interview guide about tsunamis of the mind there is a phrase, "searching for safety and higher ground, and connecting with others." It sounds as if the school counselor gave you safety at a time when you really needed it.

Lori: Yes, that's true. She is one of the first people whose caring helped me survive. And there have been many others. Some of them came into my life many years later, after I divorced and went through other tough times.

MARRIAGE

Barb: Let's go back to when you and your husband met. Did you meet in school?

Lori: This is a funny story. His sister and my mother worked together at the same company. He was 23 and just out of the army, and I was 16. He had a severe stuttering problem. In high school I had volunteered with people who had challenges. So my mother and his sister said to him, "One of these days we'd like you to meet each other."

I came home from baseball practice one day when I had a fever, and this guy was at my door saying, "I'm Ken. My sister works with your mom, and I thought I'd come over and visit." I was surprised, but I let him in. I could see that he wasn't dangerous because it was hard for him to say my name Lori. I was usually afraid of guys and would sit there like a lump. But it relaxed me because he had the stuttering problem, so we had an instant connection.

When we started going together I went with him to speech therapy at UCLA (University of California at Los Angeles). I was very supportive of him. We went together for a while, and then I got pregnant, so we had to get married. I was 17 and hadn't graduated yet. I was the only married student in the whole school so I was popular for a while. But then my friends started dropping off, and it got really lonely.

Barb: Did all of this happen in California?

Lori: Yes. We lived in Anaheim. Ken and I had a total of four children, all boys, and that was a good thing. I like girls when they're little and cute, but when they get older they're snotty! My boys had some behavior issues as a result of our unhappy home, but we had happy times too.

Barb: Earlier you had mentioned your youngest son. How old were you when he was born?

Lori: I was 36 and my other sons were 17, 15, and 11 years old. My youngest boy was a surprise, and a joy. When he was an infant, everybody in the family wanted to hold him. That was awesome in a way, although by then our marriage was pretty far gone.

My husband had had a really hard time as a child, I learned. There was a lot of anger, hostility, and abuse, especially from his mother. When he became an adult he could be charming, but with me and the kids he was often verbally and emotionally abusive. He never laid a hand on me, though. I stuck with him for 25 years, until we divorced in 2000.

DEPRESSION AND PTSD

In 1999 I went into a huge depression. My mind and body shut down. I had my first psychiatric hospitalization then. On the ward I thought to myself, "I just can't go home. I don't care if I don't have money." So I left home with only the clothes on my back. Later I went to the house one more time and got all my clothes and a few personal items, and that was all. We began divorce and custody proceedings for my youngest son, who was only 7 at the time. An older couple in my church took me in for six months.

The custody battle was a weapon my husband used against me, since he had earlier treated my son as a bother to him. But years later that conflict has been resolved, and my son eventually went to live with his dad. My ex and I are now friendly most of the time.

The year after we divorced I started having PTSD (post-traumatic stress disorder) when I was remembering my childhood trauma. The memories were devastating, and my life just shattered. I thought to myself, "I'm shattered and fragmented, and I don't know how I can ever be whole again." It's taken me 12 years of work to recover from those memories.

Barb: That's a very long time. I can barely imagine what it was like to start remembering those early traumas and then to work through them.

Lori: I have amazing friends, and a mighty God who got me through that very long road. Key people in my church reached out to me from the beginning, sustaining me and accepting me with the things I was going through. I was raising my little boy with special needs, and I was in and out of the hospital for a year. It wasn't unusual for my son to kiss me goodbye at home in the morning and then come back to find out that I was in the hospital. People passed him around from family to family from our church. I'm sad to think that my son went through that. He has challenges of his own now that I think were affected by our family backgrounds and his early experiences. I also had to go to a two-week day treatment program which helped get me over one particular hump.

I went numb for several years during that time. I don't know if it was the medication or what, but it was probably a number of things. When the trauma's too big, you just dissociate. It's something your brain does by going out of body. You go through the motions of life but you're not connected. It's like putting yourself in a cocoon where there's no pain. And that was the point where alcohol also started coming up as an issue for me.

SUICIDE ATTEMPTS

In approximately 2007, I switched jobs and was pretty healthy for about a year. Then I got triggered and spiraled out of control. One thing happened after another, trials that wouldn't let up. My son also had serious issues going on. I made a series of suicide attempts that I think were cries for help. I still had this amazing support system, some from the beginning and others more recently who were therapists, doctors, and people providing extra services.

Barb: What were the extra services that helped you?

Lori: I was at Group Health and in counseling, and I was introduced to a coping skills group. It was a whole curriculum, not just people sitting around processing their pain. It was recovery-based, focused on moving forward. They said to us, "This is the way we take care of these overwhelming feelings. These are some things you can do." That was one baby step for me. Then I took an amazing anxiety class for twelve weeks. I grew *so* much and overcame so much in dealing with my anxiety! I think that was a major catalyst in leading to my victory over my PTSD.

OVERCOMING

I made some really close friends in the anxiety class. It was a place I could gain hope and get answers for myself. I became friends with two women who had agoraphobia, which meant that they were afraid to leave their homes. But they both showed up at the class every week! Midway through the class the two women decided to do exposure therapy by going to the grocery store together. They walked every aisle in the store and picked one item to purchase. Going through the checkout stand was the hardest part, and they did it!

After the grocery store event the two women kept going on little outings together. They overcame! We could hang out together at Krispy Kreme and keep encouraging each other. All of this helped me get through my own tense feelings and start to move on. I'd been stuck for many years before that, but I'm not stuck anymore!

Barb: It's clear to me that you're not stuck. Aren't you a certified peer specialist?

Lori: Yes. I've been training to help other people with their own depression and things like that. Currently I have an internship that I really enjoy, being with other people who are trying to go forward after very hard times.

Barb: As we both know, depression can make you feel immobilized, and disconnected from everything. You have lived through that, as you've told me. But listening to you now, I can see that your experiences have given you empathy for others.

Lori: I have, and that goes back to my own stuff, both the hard times and the support for my recovery.

Barb: Lori, you are an example of how much of a difference people can make with other people. Caring doctors and health professionals help, of course. But over and over again in my own life I've had people who simply cared about me, people who reached out with love and hope.

Lori: You hit it right on the head. We need the professionals, but we have to have someone else in your life who is someone we can trust. That school counselor years ago gave me a hand-hold when she just stood there and looked at me with compassion. What a difference that made in my life! Barbara, you're one of those people too. When you and I spent an hour on the phone the first time, I could tell you had been there. My friends cared, but they couldn't relate to me in that way. You believed me, and you could see what I'd been through as I tried to get help. You showed me I could speak out and have a voice!

Now as a peer support specialist it's wonderful to be able to help others find their voice and think that they can actually *do* something.

I love the whole idea of empowerment.[13] You gave me peer support two years ago, and now I can give it to others.

Barb: When I saw my mental health prescriber recently and mentioned my book project, and she asked me, "How are you finding these people for these stories?" I said, "Well, it's just kind of happened. Some of them I've known in my local community, and one is a person who contacted NAMI Washington, trying to get help so she could stay alive. She is now a certified peer specialist, turning her trouble into something positive." She said to me quietly, "Oh - - like you."

Lori: Laughs – Un huh!

Barb: I think there are many people like us. They are sensitive people who care about others as well as themselves and family. Many of us have gone into our own black holes or hidden tunnels, trying to stay alive but to pass the light onto others. Ronald Fieve, MD, has written in his book *Bipolar Breakthrough*[14] about what he calls bipolar 2b or bipolar 2 beneficial. He encounters many clients in his practice as a psychiatrist in Manhattan who are bright and enthusiastic but also prone to depression. They have to work to stay on balance. When their brains are balanced, they can make a positive difference in the world around them. I think you and I can relate to that.

Lori: Yes! I found a church where I give and receive love, even though I am living with a mental illness. I found hope, and that is the most important medicine we take.   I heard a great quote. "You can live three to five days without water. You can live a few months without food. But you can't live a day without hope." It's true. I don't want people to die without hope.

Alcoholics Anonymous brought that home to me. I was able to share my story in a twelve step meeting, and a woman there needed to know that I have survived, that I got through it. I am so grateful. I'm getting to experience pain and difficulties in life too. I like to think of this image from when we were growing up, the little blow-up dolls. When you punch them, they jump right up. That's how I feel in my life. When you punch me in the butt I get up, because I use my tools.

Barb: What are particular tools for you?

TOOLS

Lori: The first one is that I call out to God. When I have very bad anxiety, or get some bad news, or I'm going through a trial, within 24 hours I say, "I don't want to go down this road, I need your help." I can also go out for a walk, do something fun, get moving, to get that energy out. When my mood gets down and if I feel like isolating, I try to do something happy when I get home and I'm alone. Friends make a difference in your life, but they aren't always available and sometimes they give you bad advice. So you do what you can. God's always there - - doesn't make mistakes, and doesn't say, "I'll get back to you' in an hour." That's my answer.

Barb: Those are great ideas! Thinking about how you described your childhood, it seems that there were things your parents were dealing with that were not on the surface. So my next question comes partly out of my own experience of having a mother who had depression. I'm a middle child too.

Lori: So we have a lot in common!

Barb: But I had brothers instead of sisters. My mother didn't tell me anything about sex until I had gone to church camp. I was 10 years old. One night at camp my panties got bloody and a girl in the cabin saw them and went around saying, "Look at *her*, she's gonna *die*!" I didn't know what was happening, and I was really scared.

When I got home from camp my mother said she was very sorry. She didn't think she'd have to tell me until later, since her menstrual periods hadn't started until she was 13. I think now about the cabin trauma, being kidded about wearing glasses when I was 5, and hating making mistakes at piano recitals. None of my memories seem as traumatic as your harassment by the twin girls. But for those of us who are sensitive as children, any of those things can leave a mark. So, given what you have said about your mother so far, I'm wondering if she told you anything about sex when you were a girl?

MOTHER LOVE

Lori: My mother was great about that! The day is vivid in my mind. I was six or eight years old, and I was playing with my one sister and my girlfriend. We were all together and my mother said, "Why don't we just sit down and visit?"   She put her hand on mine and she said, "I want to tell you about what it's like to be a woman." I don't remember it being about sex particularly, but it was about menstruating and your body changing so you could have a baby. She might have even done a diagram, but I don't think so. She was telling me something, with love, that she wanted me to understand. My sisters and I all remember that vividly.

I started my periods at nine or ten. I wasn't expecting it till later, and when it happened I didn't remember what my mom had told me. So I was afraid to take a bath. Pretty soon I started to get pretty ripe. My mom asked me if I was taking a bath, and I said, "Well, I have this blood coming!" So she said, "I told you what that is. Let me show you how to put the pads on, and it's okay to take a bath. You don't want to wait till it's over." She was very tender about this. It was much more wonderful than any of her failures. The older I got, the closer we got.

TSUNAMI OF THE MIND

Barb: Is your mother still alive?

Lori: No. We lost her in 2002. That was a hard time for me to have her leave. The year before that I had started to remember the early traumas, including her not being emotionally available to me as a child. I didn't bring that up, but at one point she said to me, "Is there anything you need to say to me?" When I shared what I was remembering, she said," I would never have done that. You must be remembering wrong." For me that meant that it was my fault. I'd grown up with the view that you don't have conflict. You know the elephant's in the room but you don't mention it.

I did get to see my mom six months before she passed away. Unfortunately everyone acted like things were hunky dory. I wasn't in a good place, so I endured it. It was very hard. Later, when she was on life support, I flew down to California to say goodbye. Each one of us took a few minutes to be alone with her. She was semi-comatose. I remember that her eyes fluttered open at times, but they were glazed over. They tell you sometimes that a person can hear you in that state of being. So I thanked Jesus for loving her, held her hand, and said goodbye. I had worried that I'd never told her about the richness of knowing Christ. She believed in God but she didn't know Christ. And I wanted to see her again! So I sang her "Jesus Loves Me" and I hoped that she heard me.

We were at a hotel that night, and the next morning we got a call that she had passed away. My stepdad said to us, "I want you guys over here right away." We went over to their little house, and he was in so much pain that he said to just get rid of her stuff right away. At first I was offended, but now I understand that everybody handles death differently. He came out of the bedroom and said to me, "I have something special for you." It was my grandmother's Bible! My mother had treasured that Bible.

I went back to the hotel that night and looked in the Bible. Inside was a letter I had written to my mom, one that I'd completely forgotten I had sent to her. I'd written it during a time when my mom was crying all the time and feeling a lot of guilt. The letter was meant to encourage her, to tell her about God and Jesus. There was also a poem I wrote about how Peter wants to walk on water to the Lord and has to be brought back to the boat.[15] I couldn't believe it! I thought, "This is a sign that she knew I loved her and she knew God loved her." I still had work to do, dealing with the initial trauma and the resentment and anxiety that followed. But that was a precious moment.

Barb: You remind me of an experience I had with a wonderful African-American friend I knew in Nashville, Tennessee. Annie Bell Brown sang "Amazing Grace" like Mahalia Jackson, and I accompanied her in church and in public events. She was only 43 years old and the mother of thirteen children. She was dying from the effects of breast cancer spreading through her body. Her sister Alberta had taken a bus from Arkansas to see her, so I drove Alberta to the hospital.

I had always been afraid to be near a dying person, but this was *Annie Bell*! So I walked into the Intensive Care Unit. She was breathing heavily, and something led me to sing "Amazing Grace" into her ear. I heard her make deep moaning sounds as I sang. Then I found myself saying "Annie Bell, it's okay for you to go." Her body was shutting down, but she seemed not yet ready to leave. When I left the unit Alberta went in to be with her. The next day Annie Bell passed away. I felt sure she heard me singing to her before she died. Medical people tell me that sound is heard by a baby in the womb, and it's the last of the senses to go when someone is dying.

Lori: That's also what I have heard.

Barb: So I have no doubt that your mother heard you sing to her. And I can think of no song more loving than "Jesus Loves Me."

Lori: I'll always treasure that moment. She brought me into life, and I was able to escort her out in a beautiful way. It helped me eventually to go back and deal with the resentments I had felt. I grieved immediately after her death, but I had spent a lot of years holding onto those feelings from years ago. Now I can look back, knowing that the last moment with Mom was the healing I needed. She knew in the end that I loved her enough to tell her about Jesus, and I fully expect to see her on the other side.

TIME CURE

Barb: I have been reading a book called *The Time Cure* by psychologist Philip Zimbardo.[16] It talks about some new ways to address PTSD.

A key idea in the book is that everybody has a perspective about time. It's like a little set of boxes - - the past negative and the past positive, the present euphoric and the present fatalistic, and so forth.

The researchers developed an inventory of ways people think about the past, present, and future, without using psychological words like anxiety, depression, or trauma. They were interested, for example, in learning about people's negative *and* positive past memories, not only the traumatic ones.

Lori: That makes sense.

Barb: Earlier I heard you talk about both the traumas with the twin girls _and_ your mother's positive description of what it is like to become a woman. You made it clear that you felt loved and hopeful when your mother talked with you and your sister about your body.

Lori: Yes. You have to look at both kinds of memories to get over them and find the healing.

Barb: I'm guessing that almost everyone has both negative and positive memories. We want to hold on to the positive ones and keep building on them. That's obviously something you yourself are doing.

Lori: I have far more positive than negative memories of my mother now. For many years I didn't know that I felt anything negative about her. When I did, it took a long time to process those memories and feelings. Now I'm having a lot of happy memories about my mother. The other things don't matter anymore. She was a fabulous mom.

Barb: I see that. And in *The Time Cure* Dr. Zimbardo says that medicines alone won't heal your time pictures. They can't heal your past or suddenly make you able to look forward, but they *can* help moderate some of the pain. I believe that too. I take medicines because I know from experience that I need them to stay on balance. But I also know that medicines do not make me who I am.

Lori: Right.

Barb: So each of us has a time perspective, and everyone's perspective can be different. As a young adult I had lots of what I call Mexican jumping bean thoughts. I would think to myself, "*This* will go wrong and *that* will go wrong, and it will be *terrible* when that happens!" I can smile about that now, but not then. I learned ten years ago that I have had ADD, attention deficit disorder, probably since childhood. That jumping bean energy would become toxic when I was afraid that I couldn't keep promises or get things done. Now when I see a friend who is in anguish about everything around her, I can recall my jumping bean self and have more empathy.

Lori: That helps me, too, when I am looking at what somebody else is doing.

Barb: Now back to you! When we first met, you were feeling afraid that you might give up and end your life. But you didn't want to do that. What helped you to turn around? You said my listening to you was a help, and I'm grateful for that! But were there other changes that helped turn things in a positive direction for you?

MEDICINES

Lori: From 2007 to 2010 I had Group Health, and I loved my psychiatrist. She was an incredible woman. She used a lot of the language that we use now in our coping skills class, and she encouraged me to use my recovery tools. But she also had me on way too many medications. I once said to her, "There's just *too many meds*!"

A clinic nurse met with me once a week to check on how I was doing. I was embarrassed that I couldn't think clearly at times. I had a little pill box with all the days of the week. Part of my problem was that all the pills were white! I hated to ask the nurse if she would fill my weekly pill box, but she said, "You don't have to be embarrassed. I do it all the time for people." I felt better when I watched her fill the pill box the first time. It took her about twenty-five minutes!

My eyes have been opening up about the whole medical model of mental health. It bothered me to think that I had to go to somebody to get my pill box filled! So I started to ask my doctor, "Can I get off some of this stuff?" She said, "Well, it's pretty early but let's give it a go. I want you to see me a couple of times a month." So we did that.

One my efforts to lower the number of medicines led to a problem. I'd been on Effexor for years, and the doctor told me that because of its reported side effects we needed to lower the dose gradually. When we got to the point of my discontinuing it, I started feeling like a zombie in addition to the other physical symptoms.

Between the medicines I was taking and my troubles in trying to function generally, I had a hard time working. I got and then lost several jobs in a short while. I felt as if nothing was going right, and I went into a dark hole. I don't know how much of a part the medications played in that, but I know that I don't ever want to be on that large a number of medications at once!

Right now I'm taking only two psychiatric medications. When my nurse practitioner asks me, "How are your moods?" I may say, "I'm feeling kind of funky." But I don't want to have her change my medicines automatically based on what I say in the moment. So I say to her, "If I come in and tell you about a symptom that I'm having, I'll let you know if I think it's something I can't handle without medication. But I don't want you to tweak my meds every time I have an emotional hangnail!" [laughs]

In general I haven't had things happen in the last year or two that would give me reason to go backwards. Well, that's not exactly true. I had to take Seroquel for a while when I had some paranoia and a few delusions that I'd never experienced before. But apart from that I've been pretty stable. When there's a bit of a problem she'll want to up the Seroquel, but my answer is, "No. I can do this." I think I may be teaching her something too. [laughs]

Barb: How often and for how long do you see her?

Lori: She is a mental health nurse practitioner. I see her every eight weeks, for about 20 minutes.

Barb: It sounds like this is medication management. It's not long enough for extended conversation or psychotherapy. But I think you know what is happening even if you have limited time with your prescriber. You are now your own best consultant.

Lori: Yes. I can recognize signs and symptoms of what is happening, and I know pretty well when I can get through a situation. She listens to me, and she doesn't have the approach of "I'm up and you're down."

Barb: And you wouldn't be with her if she did!

Lori: Absolutely not. I don't let people get away with that kind of stuff. I've become spunky!

SPUNK

Barb: Lori, I'm pretty sure that you didn't just become spunky!

Lori: I think I became spunky in little increments after I divorced my husband. When I was near suicide and not getting help, I don't know how I managed to write that first email to you. I guess I was pissed! My spunk just started to take on a life of its own.

Barb: When you emailed me the first time I could see that you were angry about a bad situation. You saw patients at the respite center getting worse instead of better, despite the best efforts of those running the program. You weren't so enmeshed in your own pain that you didn't notice someone else's pain. In my book, that's not only spunk. It is truly compassion.

Lori: I remember talking with you on the phone about that situation. You and I agreed that it was important for me to act on what I had observed. So I sent an email letter to the respite center director, and then she and I talked about it. I think some changes were made in the respite center's policies based on my advocacy. Others who go there now when they are hurting deeply may find it a calmer and more respectful place.

Barb: Many adjectives fit you, Lori: daughter, mother, sister, survivor, friend, worker, peer, lover of God, and spunky advocate. It's clear that you are keeping on keeping on! Thank you so much for sharing your adventure with me.

FORREST

One thing I know now is that it's not how much you can accumulate, or how you prove to everyone else how good you are. It's what you can do for other people, whether it's raking leaves, helping your neighbor, or other simple things. In the long run, you can do a lot of good for a lot of people.   - Forrest

I MET FORREST when he was volunteering at a nonprofit thrift store. The couple running the store began a local Depression and Bipolar Support Alliance chapter a number of years ago. Forrest offered to share his story with the hope that it could help other people. We had this conversation in 2013 at a local restaurant.

Barb: Thanks for having lunch with me, Forrest. Let's begin with how life was when you were growing up. You mentioned when we first met that something major happened in your family, and you were trying to make sure your sister was safe.

Forest: I was a junior in high school and my sister was younger. Our house was a place that other kids liked to come to. Sometimes they were already there when I got home from school. It seemed that my family was doing okay until my parents suddenly said they were divorcing. It was a total shock to both my sister and me. Neither of us saw it coming.

Barb: What was life like before that happened?

SKIING

Forrest: I was on my way to becoming a state competitor in skiing. I started skiing in 1980 when I was 12 years old. I skied every winter, and I went up Mount Hood one week a month. I was fortunate that my uncle, my dad's oldest brother, financed it all. He was a skier himself and wanted me to get out there. I could go 60 miles per hour through the trees on skis. That was a rush! [chuckles]

As I got into my teens my parents realized I was good at what I was doing. I did giant slalom, now called Super G, going fast and taking the corners. If it wasn't an adrenaline rush, I didn't want to do it. That would be boring!

Barb: How was school?

Forrest: I could be there every single day and still flunk the class. I knew everything that was going on. I knew everything that everybody was doing, but it was absolutely boring. So I would work a deal with the teachers, that if I came extra nights and get help, at least I'd get a D. I wouldn't flunk the class, thanks to my getting along with the teachers. I especially hated English. I took four and a half years of English to get three credits! [He laughs.]

Barb: Was school important to your mom and dad?

Forrest: I think it was to my dad. They had taken things like algebra many years ago and they didn't want to look like idiots. I don't think my mom really had much interest. For her we were more like remote controls. "Go turn on the TV." "Go turn off the TV." "Could you get my purse?"

When I'd say to her, "the purse is sitting next to you, Mom," she'd say, "Are you bad-mouthing me?" My dad was more laid-back than she was. You didn't know he was upset until he was UPSET! He spanked you but it wasn't like the beatings I heard about with other kids. But my mom could cut you with her words. It was like a knife; she didn't have to hit you.

Barb: Was either of them a drinker?

Forrest: My dad had a casual drink here and there. I had never seen my mom drink until after their divorce. My mom was dating a gentleman, and then he passed away. I remember her drinking a lot that time. Actually that was kind of fun - like dealing with a sister!

Barb: What happened with your sister when your parents divorced?

Forrest: When it happened so suddenly, my biggest thing was protecting my sister, making sure she would be OK. She totally didn't know how to deal with it. She had been the good girl. Then suddenly she was doing all the wrong things, like climbing out the window wanting to get to the boys. For me the big thing was trying to help my sister get back on track. In my senior year of high school I took a half year of night school just to graduate. But that was my option. I wanted to graduate, so I did whatever I had to do, and I didn't care where I was living. My priority was my sister being okay, and making sure she was safe.

Barb: So her world just exploded?

Forrest: It was like we hit a wall. We had been a family, and suddenly everything just stopped when the divorce hit. Then my sister met a guy and decided she wanted to get married. As for me, I looked at what was happening and thought, "At this rate I won't make it in the world. I'll be pumping gas all my life." So I decided I was going to go into the army. The army wasn't a perfect choice, but it turned out to be the best place I could be at that point. It kept me out of a lot of trouble, and away from a lot of people I shouldn't be with. It stabilized me and led me toward a career. Overall it made me a better person.

Barb: Can you tell me more about the army?

THE ARMY

Barb: The main thing for me, all the time I was in the military, was to go forward. No matter what you wanted, if they offered you a school or offered you something else, you took it, period. Doing that made me go forward into a bigger world. I don't think I would have had the experiences I had, if I didn't take those opportunities. As soon as you say no, you've stunted the growth of your career. You must take the opportunity, even if you fail at it. You didn't stop trying; you kept pushing.

When I went into the army, my family asked me what I was going to do. I didn't want the infantry; anyone can be infantry. I wanted to be more specialized. So I looked at some of the choices that would take five or seven years; that would be a long time! Then I saw one for a three year enlistment. It was chemical operations, decontamination, and being airborne. I said, "I want to do that one. I want to jump from planes!"

Barb: That would be the closest thing to skiing that you could do!

Forrest: My family thought I was out of my mind, since I had never been on a plane. But I thought that would actually make it easier. I had no reason to be afraid of it. My first plane ride was to South Carolina. Then I went by bus to basic training, and then to training for chemical operations. Then I went to Fort Benning, Georgia, for jump school.

Once I was in an aircraft I was jumping out of it, so it was easy to get over my fear. From there on I knew that's what I wanted to do, being a first responder. That's what I did with the 82nd Airborne Division. Their mission is to be anywhere in the world in 18 hours or less. There's nothing like being in the 10 percent of situations that nobody else can do. That's what I liked. I was one of the elite.

Barb: So your job for three years was to be ready to go anywhere in the world in 18 hours?

Forrest: Yes, that was my job, and I liked it! But when I got out, it was a lot like my parents' divorce, hitting a wall again. Some people can get past it and move on, but I never really got past it. I left the service for a year, because my grandmother was very ill. I was very close to her. It was more important to me to be there with her than to be deployed somewhere, and not be able to come home. So I chose to take time off to be with her, and I was there when she passed away.

Barb: Where were you living then?

Forrest: I was in Portland, Oregon. After my grandmother died, I went back into the army. I took a four year enlistment, then another four years after that. In that last enlistment, my job was in psychological warfare. That was a pretty intense period of my life.

Barb: You mentioned earlier that you got married at some point. When and where did you meet your wife?

MARRIAGE

Forrest: I met her In Vancouver, Washington. She was my sister's boyfriend's roommate. I knew who she was, had said hi and bye, but had never struck up a conversation with her. Then one day we started talking, and then it just kind of snowballed from there. I got baptized one day, married the next, and we moved to Utah right after that. That should have been a sign to tell me not to do it. But she had her three kids, and I wanted to raise the kids in a positive fashion.

Barb: I notice your saying you wanted to raise the kids in a positive fashion. In the midst of your family's divorce, your biggest goal was to keep your sister safe. Protecting other people is a big thing for you.

Forrest: Yes. I didn't want the three kids to go through any worse problems. No disrespect to her, but she had had three children with three different guys. I fell in love with her partly because, no matter which child it was, she treated them all with respect. Nicholas was 4, Jacob was 2, and Savannah was 8 months old. I hadn't thought of marrying before, but there they were. We went off to Utah as a family.

Barb: What was life like in Utah?

Forrest: I was going to school in electronics engineering, and staying home with the kids. I was doing my part. I was also in the reserves, so I went away for my yearly two week stint. I came back a day early, to find her in bed with one of the guys in my unit. I was extremely pissed! At first I said to the guy, "You have two choices; either go through the door or go through the window." He put his pants on and went through the window. Then I said to her, "I need to leave for a little bit, to collect myself after what just happened here." When I came back an hour later, she was in the neighborhood swimming pool with all three kids, and he was there too! That's when I flipped out.

My mother-in-law was in the pool with the oldest boy, and she was yelling that I was abusing the children. I had never put a hand on those kids, ever, but she was saying that I had, in front of everybody. So I said she needed to shut up, and I threw my cell phone, which hit the boy's shoulder. At that point I blacked out; I jumped in the pool and started beating up my mother-in-law. That's the stupidest thing I ever did! Four guys jumped in the pool and tried to stop me. I got out of the pool and walked away. Then the police showed up.

Barb: What were you charged with?

Forrest: The original charge was attempted homicide, from the fight in the pool, plus child abuse, and four assault charges because four people were trying to detain me. But I took a plea bargain. It looked horrible on paper, but in reality it wasn't. I'm not saying what I did was right, but it wasn't as bad as it sounded.

Barb: It's easy for me to be judgmental about someone I've never met. But it seems that this woman must have been quite appealing, to you and to other men. She must have needed affection and looked for ways to get it.

Forrest: Yes. For me, it was betrayal. I was doing everything I could to get more education, for a better life for all of us. I was trying to keep up with my military career, so I would have a pension later on. But at that point, the maintenance guy was more important to her than what I had been doing for our family.

Barb: How long ago was this?

JAIL AND PROBATION

Forrest: It was 1996. I was in jail for six months, which was actually longer than I was married. I gave her everything in the divorce. It was February when I got out of jail, and all I had were sandals, shorts, and a shirt. I decided that I couldn't live like that anymore. I had nowhere to live when I got out of jail, and I had to see a probation officer for the misdemeanors. It was weird. In Utah, if you were guilty of a misdemeanor, you can't move away without proper word through the court system. So it took almost two months before I could move back to Portland. If I had been a felon, I could have moved to Portland the day I was released!

Barb: Did you have a probation officer when you got back to Portland?

Forrest: Yes. I had three years of probation. I lived in a camper at my mom and stepdad's house, and I worked for Blockbuster. I got five movies a week that I could watch. With a new movie, I could watch it a week prior to its being released. Actually it was quite a decent job.

Barb: You said earlier that you had decided you couldn't live like that anymore. What did you decide to do?

Forrest: I first went to the VA [Veterans Administration] in Utah, to find out what was going on with me. I wanted to find out whether my actions were just stress or from something else. After I got out of jail and was back home, I went to the VA there and saw the psych doctor. I was issued medications after that first appointment. It seemed bizarre that somebody can determine a person's diagnosis on the basis of a medication working, but that's how it happened in my case. The diagnosis of bipolar was made in 1996 when the lithium was working for me.

At the time I got that diagnosis of bipolar, the label wasn't important to me. As far as I was concerned, I was okay. I figured that when someone is pressured and put in the corner, eventually you're going to break out and get upset. What you do *then* is what can be different. I knew I had a problem. I had gone to the VA to find out what's wrong, and how to do something about it.

THE V.A.

Barb: You went to the V.A. yourself. Nobody came to you and said you had to go there.

Forrest: I went to them. And I think that's probably been the turning point for me. I started paying more attention to *me*, to what I need to do to make myself happy and make my surroundings more suitable.

The point is not what everybody else wants or needs, but what I need. I think that is what changed my life.

One thing I know now is that it's not how much you can accumulate, or how you prove to everyone else how good you are. It's what you can do for other people, whether it's raking leaves, helping your neighbor, or other simple things. In the long run, you can do a lot of good for a lot of people.

Barb: Good for you! I recently heard an Oregon State senator talk in a community meeting about her own life. During a health committee session she chaired, she had said," I'm normal, and I have this situation with depression." What a concept! A person can be normal and care about other people, and also have depression.

Everyone I have interviewed for this book is someone who cares a great deal about other people. Labels like "mental illness" imply that you are separate from other people, and you care only about yourself. It's clear to me that you don't feel that way, and neither do I. As far as I'm concerned, caring about others should be the norm, although that view is not always promoted in the world.

How are things with you now, in terms of stress in your daily life?

Forrest: I haven't had a major problem in a long time. I think it's because of my military background. You could say that I'm babysitting myself. I'm educating myself about what's going on with bipolar - - what causes what, learning more about my trigger points, what makes me upset, and what I need to do at those moments. It's all about education. It's not perfect, but it has made a heck of a difference for me.

Barb: Thinking back, how does your situation now compare with what you dealt with in the 82d Airborne Division?

Forrest: In the service, you did what your instincts told you based on your training. When we were in Munich, for example, we were ahead of the line. When we came across chemical mines, or a chemical agent, we would detect it, decontaminate it, or whatever we had to do to protect everybody who was coming around it. If we came across people, it depended on the situation. If they came at us in a threatening manner, we'd kill them. If they didn't, we would detain them.

Barb: You were ready for the worst then, but trying to do all you could to prevent it. Now you try to prevent problems closer to home, along with other people in the local DBSA (Depression and Bipolar Support Alliance).

Forrest: Yes. I want to help people, along with the couple who started the group. They have put a lot of effort into helping people get better.

DOCTORS

I've had mixed experiences with psych doctors. One of them gave me 14 questions as their way of finding out about me. You mean that 14 questions are going to give you an idea of who I am? Another time someone looked at the paper documents to find out about my past, and how different medications have worked. Diagnosing by paper, or diagnosing based only on whether a medication works? A lot of medications that people are given initially turn out to be the wrong medications for them, when they are more stabilized. It's disturbing to think how much of that is going on.

Barb. I think you're right. Thomas Insel, MD, the head of the National Institute of Mental Health, agrees with you. The medications for mental health conditions are prescribed much more by guesswork than by solid science, he reported at the 2012 NAMI national convention in Seattle.[17]

Forrest: That's why it's important to me to be educated about what I'm taking, and what medications work best for me. I'm not saying that medications alone change the person, but they are part of the picture. I'm the kind of person who listens to how people say things, and how it's worded. It makes me nervous when someone says, "Well, we'll keep the medications like this for now." So you already have plans of changing it? That's not something I want to hear.

Barb: A speaker once said at a peer support event, "We're the experts on us, even if other people don't think so." It's clear that you've worked hard to know yourself, and you deserve to be listened to.

But as you know, listening takes time. A major problem in mental health right now is that there is so little time allotted to building up an understanding of a person. It takes a while to get to know what a person was like earlier in life, or to know that person when he or she is doing well, rather than struggling.

Forrest: Sometimes I think that mental health is just a business. Instead of truly trying to make me better, they're just trying to maintain, to keep the paychecks coming. That's the best way I can describe it.

As for listening, the impression I've gotten from a couple of my therapists is that they think they're smarter than me, and that they already know me before they know me. To me that is insulting. When I ask them questions, such as "What are you thinking?" they say, "It's not about me." Wait a minute! It is! "I need to know where you're coming from, and what do you intend to happen, as we are working together."

GOALS

Barb: I heard a wonderful speaker a number of years ago, at the Washington Behavioral Health Conference. Incidentally, I don't especially like the term behavioral health. It suggests that if you just behaved better, you'd be fine, rather than focusing on the brain as the source of these problems.

But here's the important thing. Talking to hundreds of mental health professionals at that conference, Dr. Scott Miller said that after a huge amount of research into what kind of psychotherapy works, they found only two things that make a difference in people getting better. First, the client experiences a real relationship between the therapist and the client. Second, the client has goals that are honored and dealt with in the therapy.[18] This is *basic!*

Forrest: Right. That is happening with me now. I started with a new psych doctor that I see through videoconferencing. He's in Portland, and I'm here. We're on a pretty good track now. It's not ideal, but it's working, and I'm happy. My goal is that I'd like eventually to have my own shop. I don't need a big fancy home, just a modest little place with a shop where I can work on cars. That's what I'm good at, making cars into something people get excited about and want to buy. With nobody pressuring me about when the car will be ready, I can do it the way I want it, and sell it accordingly. That's my goal.

Barb: I know you're working many hours for the thrift store right now. Have you been able to save some money toward your goal?

Forrest: No. I don't have any money coming in. I know I can file for Social Security and VA benefits. But my problem is that in my initial meeting with the VA, I heard that I have to admit that I have something wrong with me. That is the hardest part for me. The way I feel now, that seems like accepting failure, a failure of my own self. So that is the hardest part.

Barb: So you haven't yet decided whether to apply for disability benefits, and that has to do with what you will be saying to yourself if you do apply?

Forrest: Correct. It's a little like telling myself, "Okay, it's time to give up," if I admit to this label of being disabled. I'm not ready to say I'm disabled. To me, it says I'm not going to do real work anymore.

Barb: It's clear to me that you are very smart, and you've done phenomenal things in your life already. When you're doing all the things you are doing now, how do you think about your own brain and how it is operating?

Forrest: I know that I'm able to have a conversation of my own, and also understand that guy's conversation over there. I've got a heightened awareness of what's around me. I've been able in many aspects to excel in that.

Barb: I can relate to the idea having strong intuitive skills, and being able to tune in to somebody else's situation. When I care about another person, my awareness makes me care more. But it also costs me something, because when I care more, I can be more affected by that person's actions.

Forrest: That also means you can be open to other people's attacks. The question they always ask in mental health is, "Do you feel suicidal?" For me, being suicidal is never an option. I could be taking myself out of trouble that way, but for the people around me, the collateral damage would be a hell of a lot worse. I couldn't imagine what it would do to my nephews, to my sister, and to my parents. I can't even think that way.

The funny thing is, in combat I would be the first one to put myself through the door, not knowing what's going to be on the other side. I would do that for sure, before I'd put somebody else through that door

TSUNAMI OF THE MIND

BIPOLAR AND LITHIUM

Barb: You've had that value of compassion and caring all your life. I can see that it's basic to the person you are. One of the books I like is <u>Bipolar II,</u> by Ronald Fieve, MD. He is the doctor who came up with lithium in the 1970s as a medication to help people with mood swings.[19]

Forrest: That's the medicine I take.

Barb: I also took lithium for sixteen years, until it stopped working and I was having breakthrough depressions. A psychiatrist with expertise in medicines, Dr. Fieve invented the term Bipolar IIb. In his practice in Manhattan, New York, Dr. Fieve works with people who are very bright, capable, and energetic. The b in his definition means beneficial. That sounds like you! People with Bipolar 2b care a lot about other people, and their compassion leads them do important things to help others, when they are able to stay on balance themselves.

Compassion is a major reason I wanted to write this book. I wanted to let other people know stories of folks like you, and me, who have experienced traumas like tsunamis of the mind, and survived. We need to have more true stories of compassionate people, to offset the media images of extreme and homicidal people.

Forrest: Yes. You see it in the news: "The gentleman was bipolar." To me that's insulting. Not everybody who does a crime has that problem, and vice versa.

Barb: True. Many more people with brain disorders are victims of crime, rather than doing criminal acts themselves. But the media stereotypes can be so extreme that many people don't want to talk about their issues in public, or even with friends. People hear the word 'bipolar' and it scares them.

Forrest: Yes. And whether it's our skin color or our personality, there are wide ranges of difference in all of us.

Barb: I think I understand what you mean about having a problem with the word disabled. I was once at a big church conference where there was an invitation to people to join a committee on disability rights. When I raised my hand to say I'd be willing to be on that committee, a woman I knew said to me, laughing, "Oh, you have one of those *mental* disabilities!"

Forrest: I would say to that woman, "No, it sounds like <u>you</u> do!"

Barb: When I saw the woman later, I said to her, "We haven't talked about this before, but I have lived with bipolar depression for more than 20 years. It's important to me to be part of the solution, not part of the problem." Her expression changed at that point. Maybe it gave her something to think about.

GROUP SUPPORT

Forrest: In the DBSA (Depression and Bipolar Support Alliance) group I attend,[20] I respect the fact that we all have issues, whether bipolar or not. We can look at another person's problem from their perspective, and listen to the possibilities for going in another direction. When the meeting goes well, I enjoy it a lot. It's one place where I can watch people over a number of months, and notice how they are starting to get better!

Barb: I've visited your group, and I can see that these people care about each other. Nobody is judging anybody else for having issues, or having a problem that might get labeled. I've found that some folks listen a little better than other people; but in general, support groups are a good place to listen and learn.

Forrest: A lot of people still are in the first stage of dealing with a problem: denial. That's not to say that I am not in that stage myself [laughs]! But then the next stage is being mad, because everybody's telling you that you *are* this label.

Barb: And what do you call the stage after that?

Forrest: It's more like acceptance, when you're starting to embrace what's going on, and trying to get more information about it. That stage can last forever!

Barb: I've heard of those stages in relation to grief. They make sense here too. You can grieve the loss of a dream you had as a teenager, or what your parents had expected of you. Here's another bit of research. I read about a questionnaire that was done with various groups of people: some had unipolar depression, some had bipolar depression, and some had manic depression. There were different responses from the different groups. Those who had continuing depression all the time —

Forrest: Doom and gloom.

Barb: Yes. That group didn't notice other people very much. And in the group with manic depression, their responses were that they didn't often think about other people's views. But the third group had people more like you and me, people who self-identified as having bipolar 2 or bipolar depression. Unlike the other two groups, they reported that they cared quite a bit about what other people thought.[21] I don't think it was just what other people thought about *them*. They were more aware of other people, period.

Forrest: My problem is that I only care about what *certain* people have to say. For the rest of them, I could care less. The ones that matter are your family, your loved ones, your close friends and that. Those are the ones that make me be *me*! I can't let everyone and everything get to me, if it's stopping me from doing what I need to do.

Barb: Yes. You mentioned that it's going pretty well for you in terms of working with a therapist. I'm wondering about another thing – whether you are considering a potential relationship with another person. A number of years ago, I met someone, and I thought for a time that I might get married again. I didn't, and now I'm at a point where I think I will stay where I am. I like my home, I have my dog, and I know what I'm going to do when I'm going to do it. That's my story. But you are a lot younger than I am.

Forrest: It's still a matter of comfort. In the past I was worried about what everybody else thought about me. Back then, I bought the nicest house on the block, and had the sports cars in the garage and the wife and kids running around in the front yard. I was even concerned about how dirty the garbage can was!

NOW

The funny thing is, now I'm actually happier, having no money and living in a basement with my cat. I have had more joy in living my life this way than worrying about all my pennies, and all those things everybody else has to look at and think about. I don't have all those worries on my shoulders. It's kind of nice to be able to just do what you need to do, let things roll, just see how it works.

Next year my life could be totally upside down, but I'm going day by day, and making my decisions as they go. I feel more at ease now. My family just doesn't get it. They don't understand where I'm coming from. They ask me, "How could you be happy being where you're at? How can you be working with no pay?" To me the first priority is, does my cat have food and litter? That's what matters to me.

Barb: I can get what you're saying. I think one way that American culture is really off track is the idea that you gotta get, you gotta go, you gotta gotta.

Forrest: As if you've got to be better than somebody else. I'd rather be able to have my own garage, where I can work on my own cars. I can express myself in the customization of a vehicle, and see how somebody feels about what I've done. That's what my goal is, to see other people get excited about that car.

In the nineteen nineties, I was self-medicating with alcohol. At that time I had with me Camaros, Corvettes, any car that moved fast – the RX7s, the MR2s, all of those. Every car that I came across, if it was stock, it was _slow!_

Barb: [laughs] I love how you said that.

Forrest: If they made the car faster, I would make the car prettier. If I couldn't make it prettier, then it sure the heck got faster. What I really enjoyed was watching people's expressions when they saw little details that looked factory but had a subtle difference. When they'd say, "Ah, I really like that!" you could sell it for $1000 profit. That's what I enjoyed.

NEPHEWS

Barb: When we talked earlier, you mentioned a nephew. Do you have more than one?

Forrest: I have three. Josh is twenty two. Garrett is just twenty one, married and with a little baby; and Caden is nineteen. The two youngest ones are in college. The oldest one, Josh, is a lot like me. I think he has bipolar, but nobody's really pushed him about it. He's very good with his hands, and intelligent, but he gets bored very easily with regular books. If I gave him a book about automotive, and how to customize, he'd read it forwards and backwards and then be out there trying to show me how it was done. In his own zone, that kid is awesome. That's where he reminds me of me. I think the regimen of the military could get him into a bigger perspective other than cars.

Garrett is married and in college; he's a very good kid. He manages a McDonald's, and has been a manager for a long time. He met his wife while she was there; she quit and is home with their baby. Caden, the youngest, is extremely intelligent. He grew up with a dad who's a computer programmer, and his stepmom is a general practice doctor. This kid is brilliant, and he's going to be the big moneymaker!

Barb: It sounds like they mean a lot to you.

Forrest: I love my nephews. It hurts because they're spread out, but then again, they have to be. You know the saying;" If I stay in the nest I'm going to get eaten!" [He laughs.] I get a text or Facebook from one of them once in a while. But it's okay.

Barb: Is there anything else you want me to know?

OTHER COUNTRIES

Forrest: One thing that changed my life was seeing how people are in countries where I was in the military, in Egypt, Jordan, Saudi, Iraq, Panama. Some places were not a good atmosphere, like Bosnia, Serbia, and Kosovo. I went to Egypt in 1990, before the Berlin Wall collapsed. It was still comfortable to be an American there. In Jordan, you could only be there if you were let in by the King himself. I was able to witness how their military works, and see some of the culture differences.

All over the Middle East, I could see how people were being treated, used, and manipulated. When I'd come back to the US, I'd hear people whining about taking the garbage out, and how there's nothing on TV. But then I'd be back in the Middle East, and I'd see how quickly the simple things can change in your life.

I didn't want to be the guy with the rifle anymore. I'd served so many places where I was being ahead of the line. I didn't want to be where I could make a decision that cost somebody his life. I'd had people injured, but never anybody killed. I wanted to leave before somebody dies. That's why I left when I did. Everything was getting more complicated, more likely to require making a decision, knowingly, that somebody's going to die. For me that is not acceptable.

Barb: I'm glad you made that choice. I think the way you're living now is making a positive difference. Thank you for that, and for talking with me today.

ANN

After I started feeling better and was able to make some decisions for myself, it began to be okay to be normal, to have a quiet day. I could still sew, could still be creative, still paint, and still tear rooms apart one at a time and put them back together. Twenty years ago it might have seemed a little boring to have regular pace and normal days. Now it's comfortable.   *- Ann*

ANN AND I met in 2003 at a small group of the National Alliance on Mental Illness held in a rural United Methodist church where I was serving as a part-time local pastor. We continued to stay in touch. This conversation happened in 2014 at her home.

Barb: Thanks for this chance to visit at your home, Ann. As I've told you, I'm writing this book of stories of real and not famous people, friends who have lived through what I call tsunamis of the mind. I'm interested in what it is like for people to have lived through major personal and emotional traumas and to come through them.

Many people think that if you have a serious brain illness you'll never get better. I have also heard that if someone experiences extreme emotions or considers suicide, they couldn't be "normal people." I don't believe either of those things, and you've told me you don't believe them either. When we last talked, you said you wanted to talk about recovery. I'm delighted at that, because recovery is a major reason I wanted to write this book. Let's begin now with the time when you and I first met. You were working in mental health in a small county.

EARLY YEARS

Ann: Yes. I worked with mental health for five years. When I started that job I'd made a really big change in my personal life. I'd ended a twenty-five year marriage to an alcoholic, and I had lived with depression during the entire marriage. Actually I had struggled with depression since childhood and as a teenager. My first suicide attempt was at 16. It was unsuccessful.

Barb: Could we say 'not completed?' I see it as very successful that you're here now!

Ann: Okay, it was not completed. It's not that I didn't take enough pills; I just survived it. I had tried to get some help from my parents, but there wasn't a lot of psychiatric help available then. Strange things happened in my teenage years. I would do things that were counter to who I was and where I was going in my life. I was attracted to the bad boys, and I would do risky behavior that was not like me and not at all where I intended to be heading in the future.

I was a straight A student then. I excelled at lots of stuff, was artistic, and very much involved in the community. I was busy all the time, sleeping only four hours a night. My parents weren't really aware of my sleeping pattern, because my bedroom was on another floor from theirs. I would sleep for four hours and then do my homework, paint, and read. I had trouble sleeping and I often had nightmares.

In 1973, at the age of 18, I married after being at college for just a few weeks. I had expected to be an art major in college, but I got pregnant with the young man I was seeing then.

Barb: Did you question whether to have the baby?

Ann: Yes, very much so. But I decided to do what I thought my parents and society expected me to do. The child's father had wanted to marry me even before I went to college, but I wasn't sure. I had a lot of conflict going on inside me, although I knew I'd be a great mom. After two weeks of being married it was obvious to me that he had a drinking problem. He was not dependable, not able to keep a job, and he regularly spent all the grocery money on alcohol.

It was very hard. I thought I was mature enough to deal with it since a lot had been expected of me during my childhood. At the same time I felt incredibly depressed that I wasn't able to function well. That was the main driver for wanting to end my life. The feeling of life being more than I could stand went on for months and months, and it got worse and worse.

PREGNANCIES

Ann: During both of my pregnancies I had been euphoric. I felt I could accomplish anything. If a truck was barreling downhill to me, it wouldn't hit me because I was pregnant! I know now that I had this major fluctuation of chemicals going on within me. When the baby was born, the chemicals hit the floor. So at that point I didn't go up and down any more. All I got was down.

After my second baby was born, I started for the first time to get some help for my mental health issues. They referred to me as having post-partum depression. At that point I was grateful to be getting some kind of help, although they didn't have the right diagnosis [laughs].

Barb: Did you get antidepressant medicine for your post-partum depression?

Ann: Yes, but I still couldn't function. I couldn't take care of all of them - - the baby, the 3-year-old, and the alcoholic. I just couldn't! I was tired all day long and couldn't sleep at night. The baby wasn't sleeping at night, either. There were a lot of contributors. During that time I was offered a mothers' support group to go to. But after three or four group sessions it was obvious they weren't talking about the same thing I was talking about.

My second suicide attempt happened when my second baby was a year old and I just couldn't function. It would take me until four o'clock in the afternoon just to get the beds made. Then it would take me all night to do two loads of laundry. I wasn't seeing any way out, and I wasn't getting much cooperation from the physician. I also wasn't being really honest with the people around me about how I was feeling. It was hard to admit to myself, let alone anybody else, how bad I was feeling.

Barb: So you were thinking of ending your life?

Ann: Yes. I had a plan. I tried to get a sitter to watch the kids for a while so I could complete the act, but I couldn't find anyone to watch the children. My family members were out of state, and there wasn't anybody to care for the children. Then it came to me that I didn't trust anybody else with my kids anyway, so I was going to have to figure out how to get stronger.

FINDING GOD

It was during that time of planning to end my life that I found God. I know a lot of people will think it's strange, and that I'm cuckoo. But what really happened is that God stood at my knees, while Satan was talking to me at the same time. Satan said, "This is it. You can't do this anymore; it's time to be <u>done</u>." And God, in a very clear voice, said to Satan, "She's on <u>my</u> list." That really happened!

So somehow I dragged myself out of bed and tried to function a little bit longer. I already had a slight connection with a church family, so after the moment I described, I decided I would try to attend the church more regularly. At the church I found some supportive moms with young children. They were really helpful, then and over the years. Within six weeks of my deciding to make a permanent connection with the church, I became born again. It didn't solve everything, but I felt there was hope.

Things were tough for me throughout the 25 years of my marriage. I had wanted very much to go back to college. I dropped out 12 different times, each time after the first few weeks, because there was no support at home. After one of those times my husband said to me, "You can go to school, but you have to pay for it." That meant I had to work fulltime, raise the family, and also go to school. So it took me nine years to get my bachelor's degree.

Barb: But you did it!

SONS

Ann: Not only did I get my bachelor's degree, I also got two associate's degrees along the way. My work was mainly with young children, which I loved. I got several promotions and better jobs over the years.

Mark Twain once said about himself, "I was a difficult child, but I think my mother enjoyed it." That's the way it felt to me. Chuck, my second child, had the kind of wild energy that a part of me had, but he could also be sweet and social. I'm sure he had some ADD (attention deficit disorder) going on too, but at the time nobody was diagnosing that. Somehow we survived his childhood together.

I expected hard times when Chuck went into his teens, because I had no support from my alcoholic husband. But chemically something changed in Chuck at the age of 12, so his next few years were a snap. Fortunately my first child Scott was an incredibly easy child to be around. And he was somewhat adult-like, more logical and calmer than his brother.

Barb. So it worked well when the two of them were together?

Ann: They were four years apart. and it seemed to work. Scott was mellow, artistic, and patient, and I think of Chuck as being on top of the refrigerator all of the time! They evened each other out. Scott was patient, and Chuck always wanted to keep up and to know everything. So I got to have a lot of fun with the two teenagers when we were doing things like trips on rafts.

While the boys were growing up I also went to support groups around alcoholism. They helped me get through school and learn to think differently. It hadn't occurred to me at first to refuse to get stuck in my husband's sickness. His actions seemed to force me to be the dependable one all the time. But through Al-Anon[22] - for families of alcoholics - in particular, I started to look at my own needs and bring those needs into the picture as well. Before then the key had always been, "Keep him happy and don't do anything to ruffle his feathers."

CABIN DREAM

I was involved with AlAnon for fifteen years. When my sons were teenagers I also taught Alateen groups for youth[23] along the way. Finally I finished college myself and the kids were both in college. My husband and I went on a camping vacation that he wanted to take. Ever since I was 5 years old I had had a dream of living in a cabin or log house in the woods. When I had told my husband my dream he would say, "Someday we'll do that." We even looked at cabins on Mount Hood. I'd gather my catalogs and keep imagining living in the woods someday.

From the beginning of our marriage there was not a lot of love between us. From the start I had felt trapped. Many years later I still felt trapped, but I had obligations that kept me in the marriage. Still my dream wasn't gone. So I said to my husband, "Well, now that the kids are gone, why don't we put the house up for sale and go look for that property and build the log house?" And he said immediately, "*That's not gonna happen!!*"

I felt betrayed. For 25 years he had been leading me on! At that moment the thought that came to me was, "What am I doing here?" This was not the first time I'd left him. It was the fourth time. He'd been sober for one year out of the 25 years of our marriage. He was sober for two anniversaries one year, but then he started drinking again, and he never stopped. I had hoped that if he could stop drinking he would not be such a jerk. But when he was sober, he was still a jerk!

At that point I knew I had to work hard to keep my own thinking straight. I was not going to get sucked in and stay with him as I had done the other three times. So I started making plans to move out. I had to have a firm plan to move somewhere other than where we lived, because he would do everything he could to keep me. It wasn't that he wanted me. It was just that I belonged to him.

Barb: As if you were property?

Ann: Yes. That brings up one other story. He had bought me a minivan as an amendment gift, at a time when he was sober and making amends. He had been sober then for a year, and we had been separated for a year and a half. I had said to him, "I need to see what 90 days sober looks like." [She laughs]

So he gave me a gift. I was in my 40s at that point. It was the time he had ever bought a new car, and the first car he had ever given me. Until then I was either without a car, or I purchased one myself with money I'd saved from watching children. But this was different. We picked out a beautiful minivan, and I was really excited. He made the down payment, and then handed *me* the coupon book. The payments were going to be $350 a month!

Barb: [Laughs] So it was a gift, but <u>you</u> had to pay for it?!

Ann: That was it! So as part of my plan to leave, I sold the minivan and borrowed the car of one of my sons, since it wasn't being used. I used the money from selling the minivan to pay for an attorney! It was very scary, but it all came into place, with a lot of help from my having been in Al-Anon all that time. I was seeing a counselor at that point, and also taking antidepressants. My counselor was surprised that I had made such a drastic move, but was wholly in favor of it.

REMEMBERED ABUSE

The other major thing that happened during the last years of my marriage was that I was starting to remember childhood abuse. Memories and flashes and sounds had seemed to come from out of nowhere. Eventually, in the safety of working with a counselor, I realized that between the ages of four and a half and six and a half years old, I had frequently been tortured, raped, and terrorized by three teenage boys in the neighborhood where I grew up.

At first it seemed very strange to me that I didn't remember the details of the abuse for all those years. But over time various odd things I had done over the years began to make total sense. One of them was my memory of saying to the doctor while I was in childbirth," If I can just run away I'll be fine." Where in the world did a thought like that come from?

Barb: At that point you didn't know why you had said those words?

Ann: No, I didn't. As I look back now I think of my father as my hero. When I was 6 1/2 years old he moved our family to another state. As far as I am concerned, he saved my life! I now can remember what the boys kept saying to threaten me – "You can't tell!" It makes sense now that I would not know about those experiences for such a long time.

During the time I was trying to work through those memories, I was trying to be honest with my husband about what I was going through. I had been in counseling for a number of years, and he was not in favor of my going to counseling in the first place. When I told him about my childhood experiences of abuse, all he said was, "You know, those therapists plant memories right into your head!" That's all. There was no comfort or understanding, just something he had probably read in a magazine. So as you can see, there was a great deal of hard history that had happened before I got divorced.

When I moved, I bought property in the woods, in a place I had found and loved. My plan was to have or build a log home there. I didn't know if I'd have a job, or if I'd be accepted in the lovely old community along a river. It just felt like that was where God was leading me. I'm a pretty stubborn person. So I was ready to do things like fixing up a trailer and shoveling a gravel driveway.

Barb: Wow!

Ann: I had bought bare land, so I had to put in power, get electricity in, and install a septic system. I was doing pretty well with all these things, since I'd taken a drafting class along with my art work. I wrote down all my plans and took them to the county office. They said, "This is great. You got it right, so you can have the permit. The contractors usually give us only half this much information!"

Both laugh.

Ann: That felt good. But I was tired a lot, and very fatigued. I was still taking the antidepressants I'd taken for quite a few years, and I started getting manic. I was not sleeping well at night and I was getting frustrated because I didn't have the energy to do all the things I needed to do with my five acres.

MENTAL HEALTH JOB

Then a miracle happened. I got a really good job with the county, and that meant that financially I wasn't hurting as I had been before. I enjoyed the new job and felt I was doing well. I worked one on one with elderly people and addicts and people with disabilities. But after a while my concentration started waning, and I had a hard time doing all the paperwork for the job.

When I couldn't concentrate I'd get up at four o'clock in the morning, because that was when my mind was the quickest. As I was sleeping less and less, the depression started getting the best of me. Once again it was hard to be honest with anybody around me, and my family was far away. It had always been really hard for me to admit failure of any kind. My sons were doing well in their own lives. They would call me and come to see me often, and I was happy with those relationships. But there was something I was struggling with in myself, and I didn't want to smother them.

Barb: You didn't want to smother them because of your having a problem?

Ann: Not only that; I was feeling the isolation. I think if I'd been honest with them they would have understood, but I don't think they would have known what to do. I was seeing a counselor, but I was still having a really difficult time. Not being able to cope and hold things together just overwhelmed me. So I slipped down into a pit that I didn't think I could crawl out of, and I overdosed.

Barb: With what?

OVERDOSE

Ann: With every pill I could get my hands on. Twenty hours after taking all the pills, I was weak and trembling, but I was still here. So I was looking for the dog's prescription, just to get out! I needed to get out! I really don't remember how I got help at that point, but I know I ended up in the hospital. I was embarrassed and angry to find myself in the hospital, but I remember people at the hospital were really nice to me.

Barb: Ann, I have some memories of that time myself. As you know, I was a part-time local pastor in that community at the time you were hospitalized. I got a phone call from someone who had heard your street address on the scanner. You had the only dwelling on that road, and the local emergency volunteer report said that they had transported a person from that address to the hospital. Because of the HIPAA (Health Insurance Portability and Accountability Act) privacy regulations they were not allowed to give anyone information about where you were and how you were doing.

I knew the hospital chaplain, so I called him and he told me the words I could say to the head nurse in this situation. As I recall I said, "I know you can't verify if this is true, but if there is a person by this name, and if that person is in the hospital, will you let that person know that there has been a phone call from her pastor?" After a long pause the nurse asked me to wait a minute. Then you yourself came to the phone! You said to me that you were doing all right, and that you had suffered carbon monoxide poisoning in your cabin. You also said your sons were there or were coming to see you.

Ann: I don't remember speaking to you then. I know that I got cards and had people visit me with gifts like teddy bears. There was an element of artificialness with some of my family members who visited me. They had lived close by, but we hadn't been close for many years. I stayed a week at the hospital and I started on new medications. It was not great but it was okay, and I felt a little better when I went back to my cabin.

Nearly two years later the same thing happened. I couldn't cope, couldn't concentrate, and couldn't do my job. The money I'd gotten from the divorce settlement was almost gone, and I wasn't even close to the goals that I'd set for myself. I knew God, I attended church, and I had a strong belief system. But I *knew* there was something wrong inside me, and people around me couldn't see it. I couldn't show it and couldn't explain the trouble going on in me. It had a lot to do with the attitude I had come out of growing up, and the abuse. I was saying to myself, "I can't let anybody know. I can't think about it and definitely can't talk to anybody else about it." [She laughs]

Back at the cabin things got really bad again. I hit the bottom of the pit, and I didn't even want to try to climb out again. This time I took every pill there was in the house, including whole bottles of Excedrin. I even lost bowel control. I was extremely weak, and I was nearly out of it. The phone rang and I knew it was ringing and I wouldn't answer it. I slept for a while, and then - darn it! - I woke up. So I got out the kitchen knives, not knowing what else to do. I was so weak that I couldn't do any damage with a regular knife, so I tried to see if the serrated knife would work!

Barb: You were cutting your wrists?

Ann: I was trying to, but I wasn't doing any damage. I collapsed at the sink, got back up and crawled back into bed. After a while the pills began to work. I think it had been about 16 hours. I had been dating Sam (now her husband) for quite some time, but I couldn't call and let him see how sick I was. But I had not shown up for work, so my supervisor called the local police. They all came to my cabin, and I believe the local ambulance took me to the hospital.

At that point I was hallucinating. I didn't know if I had a job or a family or a relationship with this man. I hadn't experienced hallucinations before, and that was a big part of my fear this time. I was seeing lice on my body and on other people's bodies, and lice with blue smiley faces looking at me. I was seeing mice going in and out of a hole in the wall, and little men in the shadows. I'd never been that sick before!

When I was in the hospital this time I was taken off every medicine. Then they observed me. I was aware that I was doing uncontrollable things. I would kick the wall, even while standing and talking to someone. And when I tried to sleep there was no peace. After three or four days of this they gave me one new medication, and then another new medication.

THE RIGHT DIAGNOSIS

The psychiatrist at the hospital came to talk with me. He said, "I don't know how everybody has missed it for your whole life. You're 50 years old and you've got bipolar disorder." "What?? How can that possibly be? I work with people with bipolar disorder! I know what bipolar disorder is and I can recognize it."

But he was right. As it turned out, that wonderful old medicine called lithium gave me back my life. From then on I have not had as many highs, but for the first time my life started to be both predictable and fun. I no longer stayed up for two days and two nights doing artistic projects. But I found other ways to be creative and productive. In the past what drove me nuts was that I'd start four wonderful projects, buy all the materials, but not finish even one of them because I couldn't stay on task long enough to complete it.

I had to get myself well, so that meant I needed to quit my job, because I realized the stress of working with methamphetamine addicts would throw me over the edge. I worked well with aging people, and I was helpful with 26 year old men who thought like 6 year olds. But when you gave me methamphetamine addicts, I just couldn't deal with them.

I chose a job with much less pay, doing home care for an elderly person. One at a time was just what I needed to sustain me. I already had some education for that kind of work, and I got more. While I was starting to heal my dear Sam, who had worked in the pharmaceutical field in the past, said something that finally got through to me. "A better life through chemistry is a good way to go."

Both laugh.

Barb: I remember that old commercial. Now it fits real life, for you and me and many other people.

Ann: I'll be 60 years old next year. I might not be where I thought I would be at 60, but I'm happy. I still have goals. I still haven't built a log home, but there's a trailer and the property's paid for. And that's big thing. It's paid for and it's cared for. When the time is right, maybe we'll build a log home, or maybe we'll just have a gazebo [She laughs].

Barb: Is this the place where you have the five acres?

Ann: Yes. We still attend church in that community, and we have friends there. Right now my focus is on fixing up the 115-year-old house where we're talking, one room at a time.

Barb: It occurs to me that this house is not a log cabin, but it is a wood home.

Ann: It is our home base, and it is comfortable. I can't say that my life isn't complicated, because there's the medicine and there are doctor's appointments. And now I have a sleep apnea machine. That has helped a lot with my energy! The sleep apnea has probably been an issue for my whole life.

SLEEP APNEA

Barb: How did you find out you had sleep apnea?

Ann: It was funny. A friend of mine had surgery and asked me to come and stay with her the night after the surgery. Her family got her settled, but they weren't caregivers. She knew I was a care provider, so she asked if it was possible with my schedule. I said, "Sure, I'd be glad to do that." So, once I got her comfortable and got her pain meds ready, she slept in the reclining chair in her living room and I slept on the sofa.

When I woke up in the morning, after we had gotten up a couple times in the night, she said, "Do you know you have sleep apnea?" And I said, "What?! I don't have sleep apnea. What are you talking about?" And she said, "You snore and snore and then stop. You quit breathing! And then you breathe and breathe and snore and stop; and you don't breathe." And I thought, "Really?!" [laughs]

So I went home and said, "Sam, dear, what do I do when I sleep?" He's told me there are times when I cry in my sleep, so I knew about that. Then he said, "Well, sometimes you snore, but it doesn't bother me." And I said, "Okay, when you're awake, would you just observe?" He said he would. Then he reported this to me: "You breathed and you breathed and you breathed and you didn't. And then you snored and you snored and you snored and you stopped." And I said, "Really?!"

I went to my regular doctor and asked her for a referral to the sleep clinic. I had to do the test twice. I've had the machine now for just a week. It's hard to get used to, and it's hard not to fuss with it, but I'm getting a much better night's sleep now. And that helps a lot. I know that lack of sleep in itself can add to depression.

Thinking about my life before now, I don't know which came first, the chicken or the egg. There were many different things. I was assaulted as a child, I grew up too fast, I married an alcoholic, and I didn't have much trust in myself or other people when I was living through all those things.

CAREGIVER

Barb: That's a lot of things to live through, including different kinds of trauma. You mentioned once that you were the first of four children, and you had the job of being the caregiver for them as a child. Is that right?

Ann: Yes. But in a strange way that kept me safe because it kept me in the house. If I was helping with the baby I was in the house. When I was vulnerable was when I was pushed outside to play.

Barb: You said "pushed outside." What do you mean?

Ann: I didn't volunteer to go outside at all after the teenage boys started on me.

Barb: What were the ages of the other children in your family?

Ann: My next youngest brother was born when I was 4 ½ years old. Then I was 6 ½ years old when my sister was born. I wasn't in school yet. I had no preschool, no kindergarten, and no first grade. Our family couldn't afford kindergarten; you had to pay for it. Also, I was needed at home, to help. I was born in April, so I couldn't start school until the next fall. So I was home for my first six years and more. When we moved away, the whole school structure changed.

Barb: And the abuse happened between the births of your first sibling and the next sibling.

Also: Yes. When I was 16 my mom had a late baby. Then two and a half years later I was having my own baby.

Barb: You mentioned earlier that your first suicide attempt was when you were 16.

Ann: It was just before Mom's last child was born, my youngest brother. It was crazy.

Barb: You have told me earlier that it has always been a big issue to be able to function and to do things well. More than once you have said, "They didn't know." Did you feel some pride in your being able to keep it all together without anyone knowing how hard it was for you?

Ann: For a very long time I couldn't admit failure or defect or incapability. But something changed after the fourth time of being near death, when I was hospitalized for two weeks. For the first time I realized that to survive and do well in life, I had to tell the truth to the people around me. I had to be honest about when I was not having a good day, or several not-good days. Finally I could start to be honest about how I really felt.

Barb: That is such a big thing! I know from my own experience and have heard from many others that being able to talk with our peers is crucial for surviving and thriving in life. We've both benefited from Al-Anon and other support groups. In some parts of the mental health field, peer support is now recognized as a national best practice, equally important as psychotherapy and medications.

Ann: But none of that was offered to me between the ages of 16 and 35. There was nothing!

Barb: And that was especially hard when you had your babies and an alcoholic husband and the beginning of memories of childhood abuse. You didn't have any safe place to tell your truth!

Ann: Right. I wasn't able to say, "I'm not having a good day!" [She chuckles.]

Barb: I just heard, at a national suicide prevention webinar, that for the first time national leaders are drawing on the voices and experiences of suicide attempt survivors.[24] I thought to myself, "What?? You haven't listened to these people before?" In any case, listening to people who have survived suicide attempts will help others understand how it feels to be hopeless to the point of thinking there is no other choice. These stories matter, and that's why I'm writing *Tsunami of the Mind.*

Ann: I can't say enough about learning how to survive and do well. The pit looks so dark and so deep, and that climb up the wall looks so impossible when you don't have the energy to do it. I had no idea I had a bipolar disorder. I had not a clue, and yet I worked every day with people with bipolar disorders. And it was so interesting thing! When I worked with them, I could reach them. I could say, "Why don't you try this? I think this might help."

Those ideas came from my own experiences. I could say, "Okay, so you can't get out of bed and take care of the children and do the dishes. So let's turn on some zippy music and do it together and see how far we can get today." I could figure that out because it had worked for me! [She laughs]

Barb: I'm thinking back to the time when you were last in the hospital and the doctor gave you the diagnosis of a bipolar illness. When you were in the hospital that time, you started to recognize what you needed in order to climb up. Do you think the diagnosis helped?

LITHIUM

Ann: Yes, it definitely did. The diagnosis led to the lithium, the chemical that my body had probably needed since I was in my early teens. It makes sense that my body needed that chemical to be balanced physically. Now I know more about what had gone wrong mentally [laughs]. I didn't know about the abuse until my thirties. The twisted thinking was hidden in my unconscious because of the fear of telling anyone about the abuse.

I still had to learn how not to let my depression get that far. I had to learn how to be honest with people around me that I had not been feeling or doing well. Letting that be known was hard! I realize now that it was imperative that I be honest with people about how I was feeling. I couldn't even admit to myself until later that I had had the hallucinations. I was experiencing them but I couldn't accept that they were happening.

Barb: You couldn't accept that you were a person who could have hallucinations, because that would equal crazy.

Ann: Exactly. What I knew about hallucinations from my training in health and education was that hallucinations are way up there with schizophrenia. Good grief! I know that when I got to the hospital that last time, I was on the floor screaming for people not to touch me. I was sure I was contagious, and if they touched me they would get it! And here I had been taking care of other people! [She laughs]

Barb: I think we are all connected, with no "us" and "them." We know that different folks have different experiences, and some of those experiences are less familiar to me than others. But I don't see there being a "them," a set of crazies as separate from us "normals." I like the saying, "Normal is a setting on the dryer." [Both laugh.]

Ann: You know, after feeling a little better, and starting to be able to make some decisions for myself, it began to just be okay, to be normal, to have a quiet day. I could still sew, could still be creative, still paint, and still tear rooms apart one at a time and put them back together. And I'm glad to be here. I still consider myself a newlywed, and I enjoy our relationship. Twenty years ago it might have seemed a little boring to have regular pace and normal days. Now it's just comfortable. Using a "Happy Light" also helps when I'm experiencing depression.

[Ann's dog comes into the room.]

RESCUE DOG

Barb: You have a wonderful little dog. He was barking when he was outside, but now he seems calm and at ease being with you.

Ann: He was agitated earlier because you are new. He has a tendency to get anxious. He has his own PTSD, and he tends to overreact, towards men more than towards women.

Barb: Yeah. My own rescue dog reacts more around men as well, especially tall ones wearing caps.

Ann: Mine doesn't like uniforms. He was rescued on the freeway in California, where the dog catchers wear uniforms. When I see my dog react, I think about all the chaos I lived with for many years. The chaos just kept me going. I don't know if I kept the chaos going or the chaos kept me going. Again it's the chicken and the egg.

Barb: Yes. You're reminding me that many years ago I thought that "boring" was a terrible word!

Ann: Ah, yes. Now I notice that I'm able to sit still. It's nice to be able to know that something needs to be done, without having to jump up and do it right away. The pace is more rational [She laughs].

Barb: Ann, I'm grateful that you've been willing to talk with me about your life from across those many years. You wanted to talk about recovery and you're proof that it happens! Thank you for our time together.

DONNA

---◆---

While I was in the hospital, I became good friends with a woman who shared my tendency toward highs and lows. We both knew when either of us was getting hyper, and we would talk each other through it. I treasured the fact that we could share safely that part of ourselves.   - Donna

DONNA AND *I met at the deli counter of our local grocery store. We became friends through shared acquaintances and support group meetings. This conversation took place in the fall of 2014.*

Barb: Thanks for being willing to talk about your life with me. Will you tell me about your mother and your family?

PARENTS

Donna: My mother was a gentle, kind person. She was in her thirties when I was born. My sister is 14 months younger. Our parents were good parents, even though they both had problems. My sister was Mama's girl, and I was Daddy's girl. I idolized my dad in a lot of ways, although he was a problem when he was drinking.

Barb: What was he like when he drank?

Donna: When he drank beer he was a happy drunk, and everybody liked him. But when he went to a bar to drink, he sometimes left my sister and me out in his truck. And one major event in our family was a fight my dad had with another man. He had met the wife of the other man at a mall, and they started seeing each other. We didn't know it at the time, but my dad might have done that many times before. The husband of this particular woman decided to stop the affair. He drove my dad out of town with his buddies and drew a knife on my dad. My dad defended himself with his pointed wingtip shoes. When he got home my dad was out in the backyard, with blood going "squish, squish" as he was walking in his wingtip shoes. He told me to take Mom next door to visit friends while he cleaned himself up. He said to me, "Mom can't see this!"

Barb: So it was supposed to be a secret from her, but it may not have been.

Donna: Right. After he cleaned himself up a little, my dad did a horrible thing. He grabbed a screwdriver and went over to this man's house, where the guy was sitting in a big chair. Dad came into the room and stabbed the man with the screwdriver. The man survived, but Dad ended up in court and then at the state hospital, where they would decide whether he could be tried or not, based on his being mentally ill. I had never heard that idea about Dad when I was growing up. It was always Mom who was considered mentally ill.

Barb: What do you know about your mother's illness?

Donna: My mother was in the hospital several times for what they thought was schizophrenia. After reading up on it and talking with psychiatrists myself, I believe she had bipolar illness. But at that time they diagnosed many people as having schizophrenia. She was given shock treatments and lost much of her memory.

Barb: Had she been employed outside the home? Did she have any source of money of her own?

Donna: When I was in my twenties, she worked fulltime in hospital medical records. She kept telling her employers that she needed an assistant. She was really good at her job, but with continuing overwork and no support, she had a nervous breakdown and quit the job. In that instance she wasn't able to function, but at other times she would do well.

Our mom was more stable than my dad in some ways but not in other ways. She was always afraid that she would get caught and put back in the hospital. She had good reason to feel that way. The first time she came home from the hospital for the weekend, Dad had packed everything we owned in his truck. The doctor had said to him, "*You're* sicker than she is, and I'm not going to release *her* in that environment!" So he decided to kidnap her, basically with her blessing. My mother didn't have a driver's license, and she knew that if she had been driving she could be stopped and put back in the hospital.

Barb: Your dad didn't have that risk, because he had a driver's license. But he had heard something about himself from the doctor, and that became another secret in the family.

Donna: Right. I know now that the more times a person has to go to the hospital because of mood cycles, the more often those cycles can occur. I think that was true for my mother. After some more years my parents divorced, and my mother tried to get healthy on her own. My dad moved further north in California, but he made some efforts to stay in touch with her.

Barb: How did you and your sister cope with your mother's times in the hospital?

Donna: One way we coped with her being in the hospital was to joke around a lot. But we worried about her too. One time she was moved to a center for older people. It was basically just housing, without the services she deserved. She became anemic while she was there. She had weighed only 110 pounds when she was healthy. Mom came close to dying, and we worked hard trying to get her moved, but that could only happen with a doctor's okay.

Then a miracle happened. We met a psychiatrist who went to bat for her. He got her into the expensive hospital where he worked. She got better, fast. It was wonderful. We thought he was God! But after a week or so, we were told that they had to send her somewhere else. The private hospital wouldn't give her a free ride any longer. We felt betrayed. So my sister and I went to speak to a panel that included psychiatrists and social security personnel. We could tell our mother's story, but we did not have a vote. The panel made their decision, and Mom ended up in the state hospital again. She was in her late fifties.

Later she was released and able to go to a good nursing home. She got better for a time, but then she had several strokes. I visited her in the hospital after she had had a stroke. She was worried about us, so I told her we were doing fine. After that latest stroke she went back to the nursing home that she considered her home by that point. She died a few days later.

MARRIAGE

Barb: When did you get married, and how old were you?

Donna: I graduated from high school at eighteen, and I married Bob a few months later. I had turned nineteen when I had the first of our two boys.

Barb: You had told me that you don't remember experiencing depression before you had married and had your first child. Was having your first child traumatic?

Donna: That was part of it. I loved being a mom, and I adored my kids. But having two boys close in age was difficult. I had an enormous amount of depression when my kids were toddlers. We lived in Port Angeles, Washington, at that time.

I had a great deal of depression and anxiety all through my twenties. When I went to see my primary care doctor, he said, "Of course you have these feelings, Donna. You are living with an alcoholic." I came away from the doctor's office thinking there was nothing I could do to make things better.

Along with the depression and anxiety, I sometimes had mania. During one manic episode I was sure that if I were the President of the United States I would be able to make things better for everyone. Another time I acted on what I know as hyper-sexuality. It was a lot of fun at the time, but I was quite ashamed later and didn't want to repeat that experience.

When the boys were younger I loved being with them and taking care of them. We would enjoy going on rides together and doing other things. But when I was anxious and depressed at the same time, my driving would be fast and erratic. One particular time I was driving very fast and got to a point where there was a large gully in front of me. I swerved to the side and my car just barely hit the edge of the incline. I remember saying to myself, "This has to stop! I know I don't want to be here anymore, but I can't do this to my children."

DIAGNOSIS

Soon after that I went into the hospital, and I was given the diagnosis of bipolar disorder. My mind had been racing furiously, and I couldn't stop it. I had gone for several days without any sleep. I'd stay up and do anything I could to keep going. I finally could see that my problem had to be dealt with. I think it was my sister who came to my house in Vancouver and took me to the hospital. She had seen our mother in a manic state before, so she recognized what was going on and knew that I needed major help. Once I got the diagnosis of bipolar disorder, I started to take the medicine lithium, and for many years it helped me to stay on balance.

Barb: Were there other issues that came up when you were living with Bob and your sons?

Donna: Keeping the house clean was one of them. At first he didn't mind, but later he ragged on me for not being a neater person. I tried, but it was hard. A friend would call us and say, "I'm on my way over, and I'll see you in fifteen minutes." I would run through the house, put everything in boxes, and take it all down to the basement, including dirty dishes! I couldn't stand people thinking that I was a bad house-keeper. If I had laundry that was not put away yet, I would throw it in my closet. You couldn't believe how much you could stick in a closet!

As time went on my husband would say to the boys, "It's too bad your mom is sick. She's mentally ill and can't help it." He was the easygoing one, coaching ball with them and letting them drink beer at their after-game parties. I didn't like his doing that, and sometimes I yelled at them.

DIVORCE

The divorce process started when my oldest son was 12 years old. It went on for two years because we fought over custody of the boys. We ended up with shared custody. The whole thing was hard on the boys as well as on me. I think that I *should have* been in the hospital for some of that time, but I was able to survive and keep going throughout the divorce.

Part of the situation was that my husband had started an affair with my neighbor. She worked fulltime but also kept a nice house. After the neighbor's husband left her because of the affair, I learned that it was the husband who had been the neat one. After Bob moved in with her and her kids, their house and yard became messy. Then I realized that I had bought his bullshit about it being *my* fault that things weren't neat and clean!

After my sons and I had the house to ourselves, our house became neat inside and out. I had a chance to work in the flower bed, and I enjoyed that. In the past it would drive me crazy not to be able to find something, but now I organized one kitchen drawer at a time. Things kept improving from then on.

I had been extremely codependent, and I knew we both had issues. But my friends saw that he wasn't respectful toward me, saying, "He treats you like trash!" And I know he also went out with other women.

Barb: You had said your husband was a drinker.

Donna: Yes, he was an alcoholic during our marriage, and he's still an alcoholic. He handles alcohol better now than when he and I were together. Actually he's raising our oldest grandson. Even though it's been bad in many ways, I thank God that Bob chose to do that, because my oldest son was not able for a long while to take care of his son because of his own problems.

Barb: Back to your own experience in your twenties – It sounds as if having the diagnosis of bipolar illness and starting with lithium made a positive difference for you.

Donna: Yes, very much so. The lithium helped me for a long time.

FRIENDS

Donna: I have had two important friendships with women over the years. While I was in the hospital, I became good friends with a woman who had some of the same tendencies toward highs and lows. We both knew when either of us was getting hyper, and we would talk each other through it. I treasured the fact that we could share safely that part of ourselves.

She had been hospitalized more times than I had. She met her husband after she and I had known each other for quite a while. He was a wonderful man, and he loved her and supported her. She and I would visit at her house until her husband got home; then we'd all sit around and visit. He was protective of her but he valued the fact that she and I were close friends.

They had two little girls at a time that was somewhat later in life for both of them. Each time she was pregnant and ready to give birth, she had had to stop taking her medication, and each time she would have a major mood swing when she was without the medication.

One night after the children were born I saw her at McDonald's. She had had a super-manic time and was still higher than a kite. She poured out everything that had happened while she was on this high.

Barb: How did she sound when sharing this? Was she proud of it?

Donna: Oh no! She was terribly ashamed. She had a husband who supported her and their children in every possible way. But she had taken off and been gone for a few days. While away she had met a guy in a bar and was intimate with him. I know that with bipolar illness you can feel really over-sexed when you're in a manic state.

I knew that she didn't want to tell her husband about it. She felt terrible, like it was her cross to bear.

A few days later her husband phoned me and told me she'd died in her sleep. They didn't know the cause of death at that point, and I wondered if it might have been suicide. I have thought of her every day for years. I wish that I could find a way for her girls to know their mother through my eyes. But sadly, that does not seem possible, as they have moved away from the house where the family lived when I knew them.

Barb: You mentioned another woman friend you have known for a long time.

Donna: Yes. I've known Nancy for more than 25 years! The two of us are very different, but we have had a healthy relationship. When Danny and I met and decided to get married, she was my maid of honor. She and my other close friend worked together to make a beautiful wedding cake for us. It was the first time either of them had ever made a wedding cake!

REMARRIAGE

Barb: I have met your husband Danny, but I don't know how the two of you met.

Donna: I lived in Vancouver, Washington, for a number of years, and I went to a big church in Beaverton, Oregon. Danny and I both attended that church, and we loved the minister there. I had several friends who became friends with Danny too. He came when I was baptized in a church swimming pool, and that touched my heart.

We had a nice small wedding. I was active in my church at that time. The woman minister counseled with us several times before she would marry a couple. I knew Danny was not an active Christian, but he went to church with me often when we were going together.

After Danny and I married, we moved to the beach. Then my health situation changed, because I had to give up seeing the psychiatrist I had gone to for 20 years. The medicine that had worked well in keeping me stable for many years, lithium, was starting to cause damage internally. My primary care doctor was not sure what medication would work better. The doctor tried to change to other medicines, but it seemed that I was allergic to every other drug they tried. It was really hard, for both Danny and me.

Barb: You told me on an earlier occasion that you had gone once to a hospital in the Seattle area. What do you remember of that time?

Donna: Danny and I were living in Ocean Park. I knew that I was going in the direction of mania and needed to be in the hospital. The current medication was not working, and I knew I wasn't behaving in a reasonable way. Danny knew it also, and he didn't feel able to care for me with the way I was acting then.

Barb: Did he take you to the local hospital's emergency room?

Donna: Yes. They have no psychiatric facilities, so they checked around to see where there was an opening. The only place with an opening at that point was a hospital in the Seattle area.

Barb: Did you go there by ambulance, or how?

Donna: I believe it was by ambulance. I know I was self-admitted. I went there wanting to get healthier, and to get medicine that would help me stay on balance. But that is not what happened. I had the impression, when I first walked into that hospital, that they would get me stable and then send me home. But I found out that this is not how it works. They start the process, but they can't keep you in there longer than two weeks.

I was somewhat manic when I got there, and I was definitely still manic when I left the hospital. The doctor at that hospital prescribed a new medication for me. But they do not keep patients until they are fully stable; that takes too long. I was to be there ten days in all. I had been doing well, and it was close to the time when they were going to send me home that things went very wrong.

HOSPITAL TRAUMA

They have a structure that they put everybody through. I was fitting in, and I was enjoying myself. We had classes and were busy all day long. Then you had a group meeting at the end of the day, when everyone talked about how you were doing and how you were progressing.

Barb: What kind of staff did they have?

Donna: They were not doctors, but social workers, and people with mental health and drug and alcohol training. Our class times would focus on training you to take care of yourself. When I was either very sad or more manic, it was hard to do the right thing. I would feel like I was screwing up.

They gave you a little bit of free run of the floor during the day when you had time on your hands. I made friends with two people, and we spent a lot of our time together. I got back into my role of helping other people, which is familiar behavior.

Barb: I bet that felt good.

Donna: It felt so good! One guy came in late at night, just before we were getting ready to go to bed, and we struck up a conversation. He said he had called the hospital because he felt so bad he just wanted to end his life. It scared him; and he'd been in hospitals before. So we made a friendship bond. I know it helped him to have anybody be kind and listen to him.

I was improving some during that ten day period, and I was getting along well in general, until this one person started attacking me verbally. From my impression, she had been in and out of the hospital often.

Barb: What happened then?

Donna: She and I were going to most of the same classes during the days, and we seemed to get along well. But suddenly one day she started saying, "Stay away from me, leave me alone, and don't come in the same room with me!" Then she would proceed to follow me from room to room. It was very uncomfortable!

When I told the staff what was happening, they said to me, "Just stay away from her." I'd go into another room, and then she would follow me in there, and then she'd start harassing me, and I couldn't get away from her.

I went to the counselors and told them what was going on, and they said, "Just try not to go in the same room she's in." They finally said they would go and talk with her, but the problem continued. I finally went to them and said, "If you have to separate us, that's fine with me.

I just want it to stop." I know I raised my voice, since I felt I wasn't being heard. So they put me in isolation. I agreed because I didn't have any better solution.

Barb: What was the isolation like?

Donna: It was two rooms with a big window, so they would watch and hear me and observe my behavior. I felt threatened being there and I got more and more upset. There was a bed in one room, and a second room with only a table in it. The only private space was the bathroom.

Barb: There was no sofa or chair in either room?

Donna: No, just a bed in one and a table in the other. During the night someone said they were going to remove the table, and I felt even more threatened, as if they were treating me like a bad person. But I wasn't!

Barb: As if you were being a danger?

Donna: Yes. My mood progressively got worse. I felt they had no reason to take the table away. It was here when I came in, and I wasn't doing anything with it. I felt that was the last straw of being treated like a person completely out of control and not being listened to, after eight days or more of my being a helpful and cooperative patient.

Barb: Were the people who came into the room with the table counselors, clinical staff, or security?

Donna: At first it was one of the counselors. Then it was security. When they came in to take the table, I held onto the table. I didn't want them to take it. They enlisted more help, and other people came in and were trying to get me tied down. There were four people in all with me on the floor. They put shackles on both feet, and put my hands behind my back, also with shackles, and a chain tying the legs and the arms, so I couldn't move at all. They lifted me onto the bed and left me there for a period of time; I'm not sure exactly how long.

It was overnight, and I did not have my own clothes or other possessions with me. I felt as if the staff, people I'd been getting along with really well, suddenly were against me.

Barb: And the other woman was not on the scene.

Donna: No. I had raised my voice about my frustration with that woman, and I had said to them, "Do whatever you want to do." That's what led to me being put into the isolation room.

Barb: Some of what you describe doesn't make sense as a way to work with a person who has manic depression or bipolar disorder. You said some of the staff people were drug and alcohol professionals. When you came to the hospital, were you drinking?

Donna: No. They knew that was not the issue. I think the woman who was harassing me was also there for mental health reasons. Whatever her problem or issue, I didn't want to keep being exposed to that.

Barb: This is just a thought. What you described sounds like someone living with a borderline personality disorder. That illness can seem in some respects similar to a bipolar illness, but it tends to develop from extreme early abuse and neglect. Over time you feel like you have to hold tightly onto one person, to hold on for dear life, so to speak. If that person is not willing to be your total friend or partner in life, he or she becomes your enemy, and there's no middle ground.

I know it's very hard for other people to recognize and treat effectively someone with borderline personality disorder. If this woman was at first your friend and then told the staff you were a dangerous person, the staff might have had a hard time figuring out what was going on between the two of you.

Donna: The fellow who handed out the medications was very friendly with me before all this happened in the isolation room. When they came rushing in, he was one of the ones who held me down on the floor, completely different from his earlier actions.

Barb: That must have been hard! Your experience makes me think of solitary confinement. The worst thing you can do to a person is to put them where they have no link with anyone else, no chance to do something constructive, and no chance to think of themselves in relation to the outside world. What makes people think that this would lead anybody to get better?

After the staff held you down on the floor, what happened then? You had said that you had admitted yourself to the hospital.

Donna: The staff tried to persuade me to leave the hospital. And at that point, I thought, "Yeah! I will definitely go home." But it was in the middle of the night, and they made clear that they wanted me to leave as soon as possible. Danny couldn't drive there until the next day, and I knew I was still definitely having issues.

Barb: The hospital said at first that they couldn't afford to keep people until they were stable, but would help you get as far along as possible. But that wasn't working, right?

Donna: Right. I'm recalling this as well as I can. I walked down the street to a restaurant, to wait until Danny could come and get me. My head was not in a good place. The fire medics and police came into the restaurant and talked with me, saying, "Okay, just take care of yourself and everything will be fine." I recall later being in a store, and I believe I had an issue with one of the customers and myself. The police and firemen came back, and said, "If your husband doesn't pick you up and leave with you, we're going to have to arrest you." Fortunately Danny came right after that and took me home.

Barb: Had the hospital staff left medicine or a prescription with you?

Donna: I think they sent some medicine with me, and it was one that didn't work to help me get more stable. I got progressively worse when I was in the back seat of the car with Danny. He had brought a friend with him so he wouldn't have to deal with this by himself. The friend was in the back seat with me. I put my hands on Danny's shoulders, and got right up in his ear and told him how rotten he is. I acted terribly, and I felt a lot of remorse about that later, since it threatened our marriage.

Barb: This whole event is an example of being re-traumatized rather than getting the help you needed to deal with the trauma you had already experienced. In twelve-step groups they talk about HALT, the four elements of risk if we are Hungry, Angry, Lonely, and Tired. You experienced all of those together, along with being judged and put in isolation.

Donna: It just didn't seem at all fair, and I know my behavior got worse at that point.

Barb: So what happened when you got back home? Did you have someone knowledgeable to talk with?

SISTER SUPPORT

Donna: My sister was a big help. She lives in Oregon, and lives in the wintertime in Mexico.

She has been my advocate for many years. She understands my illness better than anyone else. She came here right away, saw what was going on, knew that I needed professional help, and was very persuasive in getting me into the local mental health center. She arranged for the counselor assigned to me to observe me at home. That helped get me through the waiting process sooner and be able see the psychiatric nurse who prescribes medicines very soon.

Barb: It's so important that your sister understands you as more than your illness. As all of us know, these illnesses often come from things that happened in your brain long before particular symptoms turn up. As a musician, I think of her knowing more of your symphony, more than a couple of French horns or saxophones. And you know more about yourself as a whole, too.

After that first traumatic time in the hospital, I remember seeing you when you were having major hand and mouth tremors. It was clear that these physical changes were worrying you. Because those problems were getting worse, I recall that you had Danny drive you to the hospital in Longview and asked to be admitted. What was it like going into that hospital and self-admitting?

Donna: I felt like I had a little bit more control. I knew I was ill and needed help, and I wanted to do what I could to get better.

While I was staying in that hospital, a new doctor came through in the evening. She said, "I'll see you in the morning. I'm going to be your doctor for the weekend." She came back the next day, and I could tell she had read my file. No doctor in a hospital had ever done that before!

I was impressed with that. But she was not local; her office was located an hour away in Olympia. I had tried to get a doctor in Longview or in Vancouver, but there were no openings. She asked the head of the department if he would make an exception and take me on as a patient. She brought him into my room and we talked. His answer was, "Right now we don't have anybody in Longview; but we will have a new person coming on in a few months."

Barb: As if to say, "Just hold on, and don't get moody for a few months!"

[Both laugh.]

DOCTOR SUPPORT

Barb: You told me that the psychiatrist on call took the extra step herself.

Donna: Yes. She said, "Donna, you are a good patient! You have been taking care of yourself very well for many years. You are an exceptional patient, and you need an exceptional psychiatrist. Regular doctors, and even mental health nurses, don't know enough. It takes much more time to become a psychiatrist."

That impressed me. I thought about that, and I realized, "I *am* a good patient! I work really hard to be a healthier person." That includes the time after we had come to the beach and there was no doctor with the expertise I needed.

I've been going to this new doctor now for more than a year now. I continue to be grateful that I have found her, even though it can be hard to reach her at times. The medication she prescribed for me, clozapine, is one I didn't realize was out there. When I started with it I had to have blood tests every week for a few months, and now it is every two weeks.

Barb: Is that the only medicine you have for bipolar?

Donna: No. I have other medicines, but this is the primary one that has helped me to stay stable. During the first year with this new medicine I called her every week after I got my blood test, and she wasn't paid for that.

Barb: This doctor's attention and dedication to your wellbeing are impressive. She went from being the on-call weekend doctor in the hospital to agreeing to take you on as her patient. The fact that she read your file means that she may know about your prior hospital stay, which was the opposite of healing. She knew you, and she said, "You matter." All of us need to have someone who says to us, "You matter!"

Donna: Yes. She is a human being, and she and I both have our quirks. So far we've been able to work through those little irritations. [Both chuckle.]

Barb: I have mixed feelings about having encouraged you to tell me the story of your ten days from hospital hell! What happened to you was, on the whole, not of your own doing. It is clearly not how things are supposed to be when a person comes to a hospital to get better. I believe that when and if it's known and recognized that these traumatizing events can happen, that there is less of a chance that they will happen in the future.

Donna: Yes. Some of the healing just takes time. I had been proud of myself for not slipping further into my disease. I knew that the things that happened the last night at the hospital shouldn't be happening to anyone.

Barb: The more we know what others are dealing with, and how complex we are, the more chance there is that all of us will become better listeners, whether we are friends, family, or health professionals.

Donna: Currently I still spend a lot of time when I'm home lying on the couch and watching television. I'm not proud of that, but it's where I am right now. It may be depression; I know I'm not as active as I was a number of years ago. Watching television is much easier than pushing myself.

Barb: It seems like your knowing yourself is important, since your first responsibility is to you.

Donna: Yes. And my husband is doing much better at taking care of me than I had first expected. He's grown through all of this too.

Barb: It sounds as if you both are growing.

Donna: I've learned that the more often you have episodes, the easier it is to have another one.

Barb: I believe that the brain has these circuits, or grooves. When there is a groove it acts like a path that becomes deeper over time. It's like a car or a bicycle going down repeatedly into that same place in the path and building a rut. That's a little scary. But knowing about how my brain acts allows me to know more about how things happen over time and what I can do to stay healthier.

Donna: That's been my experience.

Barb: Thank you, Donna, for taking this time to share your story.

JIM

It helps me to know that there's something going on in my brain that's not quite right. With work it may not be able to be fixed, but I can learn to live with it better. A lot of it is being able to understand. — *Jim*

JIM AND I met at a support group meeting in January 2015. He was discouraged when he first came to the support group, but over the next several months he became more hopeful, and more involved with other people. This conversation took place at my home in August 2015 and in January 2016.

Jim: When I went into the mental health center here, I was very suicidal. I was saying to God, "Please take my life. I just want to be through with life." But I didn't have a way of doing it. I was afraid to eat pills and become a vegetable, so I thought I would just step out in front of a truck. But I was afraid of what it would do to the driver! [He sniffs.]

Everyone's been telling me that they would help me. But I said to them, "I don't need any help. It's just me."

Barb: Meaning that it's just who you are?

Jim: Yeah. I went in and said to them, "Guys, it's up to you if it works or not. This isn't fun."

Barb: What was fun when you were a kid?

Jim: Fun was the carousel downtown, where there used to be real ponies. I always wanted to ride those ponies. I thought that if I rode those ponies, I'd be a cowboy. I had a little cowboy hat and got on the pony, and I went around in a circle waving. That was a good time. But I look back to the rest of my life, and there weren't any really good times. What I had thought was fun was really never fun. When I got into the drugs and alcohol, I thought those were good times, but now I know different.

I wasn't happy, but I had to paint that picture for everybody.

PARENTS

Barb: What can you tell me about your parents?

Jim: My parents met when they were both patients at Western State Mental Hospital. My mother had already had three children, and was divorced. While she was in the mental hospital, her older kids stayed with their grandmother in Ilwaco. My mother was musical and played piano, but she also had manic depression. She once ripped out the stairs in her mother's house, because she didn't like where they were located. It took her just a few hours to complete the job. She had been told not to have more children, because she might die giving birth, but she had four kids with my father. I'm the last of her seven kids.

My dad was mean. He molested one of my sisters from ages eight to fourteen, and he announced it one night at dinner when he was mad at my mom. He was a hardworking logger who used a crosscut saw until he finally started using a chainsaw. He was set in his ways. He beat my mother often, and he shot at us kids with his rifle when we were outdoors. We learned how to run zigzag, so he wouldn't hit us.

One thing my dad did left me feeling guilty to this day. A neighbor dog would come over and jump up on me. I was scared, and I cried. After three or four times, my dad kept the dog at our place and said he was going to kill the dog. The man's wife heard this and told him, "That crazy guy across the way says he's going to kill the dog." When the man came to retrieve the dog, my dad had my brother Robbin go inside to get his rifle. When the man said "You can't kill my dog," my dad said, "I'm going to kill you instead." He raised the gun, and my mom hit the gun. The shot hit the guy, but it didn't kill him. I was in school the next day along with the guy's kids. I felt bad, and I thought it was my fault. I thought my dad loved me so much that he would kill the dog for me!   My dad went to jail and then to prison for the shooting.

When my dad was in prison, we moved from Amboy back to Ilwaco, and we lived at Granny's. It was 1967, and I was in third grade. I had an eye test at school, and they sent home a note pinned on my shirt, saying that I needed an eye exam. At the hospital in Longview, the eye doctor told my mom I had some brain damage, and glasses wouldn't help my eyes. I might act and think a little different than other children.

I had trouble doing the new math that year. At the end of the year, the teacher told Mom I could do third grade again or go on to fourth grade. My friend Tommy had failed an earlier grade, so he was going to be in the third grade too. Mom left it up to me, so I stayed in third grade along with Tommy!

Barb: You wanted to be with your friend.

Jim: Yeah. That year and fourth grade went okay. But the summer before fifth grade, I learned about marijuana from my older brother. That was really cool; it made you giggle and made you hungry. So in fifth grade, I introduced a few of my friends to marijuana at lunch time. Many years later, some of them still say to me, "You're the one who got us started smoking pot."

I also stole money from people across the street from us, though they didn't know I had done it. The couple was getting married, and they were going to sell us their house, so we wouldn't have to rent any more. My father was still in prison, but we kids got Social Security from him, so we were able to buy the house.

Mom and my stepdad would go over and have a drink with them. Once when they were in another room, I reached into her purse, opened up the wallet, and took out a bunch of twenty dollar bills. When I got to school the next day, I gave twenty dollars to each of my friends. The mom of one of them found the bill in his pocket, when she was doing laundry. "Where did you get this?" she asked. "I got it from Jimmy." I lied to my mom, and said, "I found it." My mom asked our neighbor if she was missing any money. The neighbor had no idea that I'd taken money from her. Mom kept asking me, and I finally said I had gotten it from Hazel, so then I was in trouble!

TROUBLES

During the fifth grade, I started seeing a psychologist. The school had said to my mom, "You need to get some counseling for this kid." But I was told *not* to tell the psychologist about anything that was happening at home. That was the same time that my stepfather started molesting me. That went on for a while, but I tried to block it out mentally.

I got in a bad car wreck when three of us guys were on our way to another town to get some marijuana. My one friend was driving very fast, and I was in the back seat, when we hit a rock bank. When the car crashed, it flipped once, rolled five times and slid 250 feet on its top.

My leg went out the window, and I got out of the seat belt. I was able to get the driver out by pulling his arm free. His hand was pinned to the steering wheel by the top of the car. People drove by and thought everyone was dead, but we had survived.

After the accident, I was in a cast that went up to my hip and around my foot. I was homeschooled by a friend's mom, because I couldn't get to school. I went to work with my stepdad cutting scrap iron, and he molested me on the way there and back. When I told my mom about it, she didn't believe me.

At that point I got quite rebellious. When we were at a wrestling tournament and taking a break for lunch, something happened that made me look at my mom and say, "Fuck you, you bitch." My stepdad said, "We're going home." I said, "You're fucking right we're going home!" When I got home, I got a club I made at school in woodshop class, and I tried to beat him to death, but it didn't work.

Barb: Did you hurt him a lot?

Jim: Yeah, but he survived. Many years later, my stepdad also molested my niece. When I heard about that, it brought everything back from my own times with him. I thought I should've killed him. My niece and her mother, who's my sister, also don't talk about these things. My niece feels like I do, that her mother didn't protect her.

RESTAURANTS

Jim: When I was 12 or 13 years old, I started working as a dishwasher at my friend Gordon's cafe. He taught me how to cook. I learned how to do hamburgers and eggs on the grill, things like that. I wasn't a cook officially, but when they'd take a cigarette break, I would cook. When I was away for a while, Gordon had leased the restaurant to a man named Jim. When I came back to town, I told Jim I had worked for Gordon before that, so Jim hired me.

Gordon doesn't drink; he's a sober alcoholic who makes really good marijuana cookies and brownies. One Saturday night when Jim was in charge, I did my usual eight hour shift. Then Jim asked me to do another eight hours. After that shift was over, Jim said he needed me to do another four hours. He put down a bindle of cocaine so I would stay awake. I went home after the twenty hours, took a shower, lay down to take a nap, and when I got up it was four hours later. I was supposed to take only a two hour break. When I walked into the restaurant, Jim fired me!

I waited till Monday noon, the busiest time at the restaurant. I went up to Jim at the cash register, and shouted, "Hey! I want my check and I want it now! In fact, your check's no good; give me cash." Gordon and his wife were having lunch at the café that day. Gordon called me over, and I told him what happened. "How are you going to survive?" Gordon asked me. "I don't know." So Gordon said, "I'm going to hire you right now. I need the place painted and the grass cleared. Are you hungry? Sign the ticket." I said, "Okay." So Jim couldn't kick me out, because I was working for the owner and painting the place.

Then Gordon told me that Jim was two payments behind in his lease. There was a clause that if the person leasing it missed three payments, it went back to Gordon. I wanted to help Gordon, so one night I went after closing to steal the money from the till. I unlocked the restaurant, but then I got scared and left. I went to a couple of bars, had a few drinks, and told my pal what I was going to do. He said, "Oh, let me do it." I told him how to get in, where the bank bag was, and to take the whole bag and not leave any fingerprints. But we both got arrested. I took the rap for it, because it wasn't my pal's idea; it was mine. So in my trying to help Gordon get his restaurant back, I ended up in prison.

PRISON

I was 21 when I went to prison. I'd been in jail before as a minor in possession, and various other charges. I'd have to sit in jail for a while when I couldn't pay the fine. This time was different; it was prison. I was there for eighteen months.

When I got to the prison, I was stripped naked, and I sat waiting till they would give me sheets, a blanket, a pillow, and coveralls to wear. I was told which cell to go to, and I walked a long hall – it seemed like a quarter of a mile – to get to my cell. When I got there, three big guys were playing dominoes. One looked at me and said, "Do you have any sisters?" I threw down my stuff and grabbed the head of the biggest guy, to show them I could take care of myself. After that first fight, the one guy said, "Bro, you're gonna do all right." I said, "I ain't your bro." I knew I had to fight to survive every day for eighteen months.

When I got out of prison, I decided to show people *the real me*. I was going to be an asshole, instead of the caring person I had been as a kid. I drank day and night, and I got in a fight every day. I was staying at the Broadway Hotel in Longview, owned by my friends Ron and Carol. After one of my fights Ron said, "Jim, one more fight and you're out." I went to the bar to think about it, came back, and got in a fight with Ron's oldest son, who hit me using karate punches. I was knocked out seven times, and I was finally able to break his leg. I knew I was done for, when Ron came to see me the next morning. But Ron surprised me and said I could stay. He said, "David knew he was not ever to use karate; you taught him a lesson." But Ron also said to me, "Jim, this new guy isn't you."

When I was still in prison but on work release, I had a furlough from the work camp, so I went to Gordon's Longview restaurant. He saw me and said, "Oh, wow, you're out!" I said, "No, but I can get out." "How do I do that? I want you here!" He wrote to the superintendent of the work camp, saying he had hired me, so that got me out of prison and into work release. I didn't actually have a job yet, so I sat around the restaurant till Gordon fired a cook and hired me for real.

Barb: Gordon was quite a friend!

Jim: Yes, he was. He was fifteen years older than me. I lost track of him after I left the restaurant in Longview. I've tried looking him up on the computer for old time's sake, but no luck.

All my life I was a people-pleaser. I would do anything that someone asked me to do. My family said that I was crazy - "crazy stories," "a character," they said. That's what I thought I was. To them I was happy-go-lucky. I didn't share anything about the bad things in my life. I tried to cover them up and be happy, but inside I wasn't happy.

LORI AND BELINDA

When I was in my early teens, I met and liked a summer girl visiting the peninsula. I kept her name and number when I was in prison, but when I got out and couldn't find her, I threw her number away. Later on, at a local bar, I got to know two girls who lived together. I'd go out with Donna, have drinks and smoke pot. One time I went to their apartment and looked at the mailboxes that said Donna and *Lori*. I suddenly realized it was Lori from years before - - the love of my life! So I knocked on their door. When Lori answered, I planted a big kiss on her, saying, "Where have you been all my life?" She said, "Are you crazy?" So I said to her, "You and I used to go down to Long Beach and smoke pot behind the police station."   "You're *that* Jim??"   So that was the end of me and Donna.

Barb: How many years was this after you first saw Lori, since she didn't recognize you?

Jim: Eight years. She was 13 when I met her, and when I saw her again she was old enough to go to a bar. Lori and I were together for seven years, and we had two children, a daughter and a son. Lori had schizophrenia. She would take her meds and then go off her meds, and then she'd end up in Western State Mental Hospital. When she'd get out, it would be good for a while, but then she'd have to go back in.

Barb: So you and Lori were together, when she was not in the hospital?

Jim: Yes. Our daughter Belinda Nicole was born when I was in prison in Clark County. When I was in prison, I fought for custody of her. I was granted visitation, but I was incarcerated in one county and the visitation order was in another county. So I wrote the judge about it, and four days later I got a visit from my daughter!

I went to an alcohol program, and also to parenting classes that were required by CPS (Child Protective Services). I flunked the class twice because my child custody hearing would be at the same time as the parenting class. After the third time of the class conflicting with the hearing, the parenting teacher decided to go to court for me. The judge said, "We'll give you your daughter, but you have to leave Lori."

Barb: That must have seemed unfair.

Jim: Yes it was unfair, because Lori had never hurt Belinda when she was with her. But my first priority was to see my daughter.

When Belinda Nicole was little, I saw her on weekends. At that time I was working in Port Angeles doing phone solicitation, selling circus tickets, light bulbs, and variety shows. I would earn a hundred dollars a day, then go to the Seattle racetrack and buy food, cigarettes, beer, and bus tickets down to Longview and back. Every other weekend, I caught the bus to Longview on Friday and stayed in a motel. I put everything from my apartment in storage, and I kept Belinda's crib stored in the motel's linen room. The motel owners were cool people, and they understood that I would rent from them every other week.

My daughter loved her daddy. During our visits, I'd get down on the floor and play ball with her. When I was told, "The visit's up," they would have to pull my daughter out of my arms. She was an angel when we'd go out and eat. If I said "No" about something, she wouldn't do it again. Once she got out of the booster seat and went over to somebody else's table. When I said, "Belinda, you're not to do that," she said, "OK," and got right back up in the booster seat. She didn't eat candy, sweets, or soda pop. They had just come out with cheese sticks, and she liked them. Trail mix was another favorite of hers.

When I applied to the court for custody, I was told, "We can't give you custody, because you don't have a home." I told the state people, "The minute you tell me I have custody, I'll have a home. There's no reason for me to have a home when I have only two weekends a month to see my daughter." It seemed just one more way for them to keep me from having her.

Finally we threw in the towel, and we let her be adopted out. I wanted my friends Ron and Carol to be considered for being Belinda's adoptive parents, but she was sent instead to another family living somewhere outside Longview. They don't know her family history, including her early seizures, heart disease, diabetes, and mental health stuff that runs in my family.

Barb: Did you see Belinda when she was having seizures?

Jim: Yes. They thought it was something she'd grow out of. She'd go limp, and then be dizzy for a while. It would last five to seven minutes. Sometimes it happened when she was with me, and sometimes after the visit ended. The officials thought it was because of being with me, but I said to them it was a reaction to her having to leave her dad and go back to the other place!

Barb: Something occurs to me from what you describe. I've known an older woman who would act in a similar way after a family visit. The nurse told me it can be a vagus nerve response. The vagus nerve runs from the back of the head down through the intestines. It is the largest nerve in the body. When there is stress, including positive stress, the person can become unconscious all of a sudden. It's just a thought, but who knows?

How often have you seen Belinda since she was adopted?

Jim: The last time I saw Belinda Nicole was in 1986. She was born November 21, 1984. Assuming she is still alive, she is 31 years old. I was told she lives somewhere north of Longview, and that her name is similar to her original name. I've looked and looked for her, but I don't know where she is. I think about her all the time.

My son Joshua Bryant was born when Lori was back in Western State Hospital. When she gave birth, he was taken to a hospital in Tacoma. I let him be adopted this time, because I wasn't going to put him through what my daughter went through. In 1989 Lori and I were no longer together. She went back into Western State Hospital on an attempted murder charge. A man had raped her, and she had tried to kill him with a butter knife.

Barb: You've mentioned Ron and Carol. How did you first know them?

Jim: When I got out of prison, I was in work release. Just up the street were the Broadway Hotel and the Greyhound Bus Depot. Ron put me up there for a year and a half, and we have stayed friends over a lot of years.

TRI-CITIES

After I had done the phone work in Seattle for a while, I decided to go east to the Tri-Cities to get away from the cocaine and heroin. When I got there, I was surprised to find that Pasco in the Tri-Cities was where all the dope was coming from!

I moved into a motel, and one night I got a wrong number when I tried to call the manager. A woman answered, "Child Protective Services –" I said, "What the hell? Are you open this late at night?" "No," she said, "We're an answering service."

So I talked with this gal for twenty or thirty minutes, and finally said, "So, are you married, or – tell me about yourself."

[Both of us laugh.]

She said, "I'm a single mother of two, and I work for this answering service." I told her I was new to this area. She said, "I'm from South Dakota. I went to college, am in debt up to my ears, and I haven't been able to put my college computer work to use."

I gave her my phone number, saying, "Give me a call, and maybe we can get together sometime." Two days later my phone rang. "Hi, this is Deanna. You remember me from Kelly's Answering Service?" "Yeah, you answered as Child Protective Services." Then I told her my story about why I hate CPS. We continued talking on the phone for a couple of weeks. Then she said, "I'm a little bit overweight." I said to her, "That's okay; people are people. They come in all shapes and sizes and colors. Do you know how to cook? I haven't had a home-cooked meal for ages."

"I'm a good cook," she said. I replied, "Never trust a skinny cook; they don't taste their own food." A few days later she invited me over for a dinner of chicken fried steak, potatoes, and corn. It was *gooood!* After being at her house, I felt guilty and said to myself, "I've gotta quit this dope. She's got two little kids, and this could turn out to *be* something."

So I set my mind to quitting the dope. Instead of the heroin I started drinking whiskey. I'd drink a fifth before I went to her house, and I'd take a fifth over with me. We'd have a couple of drinks at her house, and then I'd leave the bottle there. Soon I was down to a fifth a day, and after working on it, I was eventually down to nothing. After two months, I told her that I still have the urge once in a while, but I've kicked it.

After we had gotten together, Deanna got a job with the Kennewick Police Department. I had a neighbor in Pasco who went to auctions, and he showed me the neat stuff he got. So I went to an auction, loved it, and started going there every Tuesday. A guy named Charlie asked me, "You want to help on the floor? You do one side, and I'll do the other side."

AUCTIONS

I worked with Charlie for two months. The owner/auctioneer named Dave asked me to take in consignments and set things up at his Kennewick auction. "I can't pay you much, but I can give you one or two percent of the gross." I worked at that auction for four months. Then I was asked to set up an estate sale for him. I told him, "I've never done an estate sale. But you tell me what to do, and I'll do my best." The estate sale brought in about fourteen thousand dollars. Now I had money in my pocket, and Dave had sold me the Kennewick Auction.

I said to Deanna, "Quit the job at the police so we can run the auction." I found a bigger building, and we had that auction for about a year. Before I bought the Kennewick Auction, I had met Tammy and her husband. They would come there, and he would consign. I let them stay at my place, and then I bought an Airstream trailer where they could stay.

Deanna and I were disagreeing about whether to change things at the auction. At one point she said, "I can run it better by myself than you can." Then one night, Deanna's daughter saw me in the pit room of the auction kissing Tammy, and Deanna's 14 year old daughter said in a whisper, "I wondered how long it would be before the two of you got together."

At that point, a friend named Chuck asked me if I wanted to go with him, to buy storage units in Portland. I told Deanna I was taking my truck and going with Chuck. The next morning I met Tammy at the gas station, and we started off for Portland, leaving the others behind. Deanna and Tammy's husband tried to find us, but they had trouble along the way, and they didn't catch up with us. Tammy and I finally went on to Longview.

After Tammy and I had gotten set up in Longview, Deanna called to say she was going to sell the auction for a thousand dollars. I said to her, "No, you're not!" I went over to Kennewick, sold the auction for five thousand dollars, and paid off Deanna's bills. Deanna and I are friends now. We just weren't made for each other.

Tammy's husband called me once and wanted to go somewhere and fight. I said to him, "Let's meet in a field, and then have a drink with whoever wins." He was a good worker, but he'd go all over five states to get ten pills, and no doctor would prescribe anything for him. He couldn't get over what had happened with me and Tammy. He has since passed away.

Barb: So you and Tammy lived in Longview for a while, and then moved east.

Jim: Yes. We went back to eastern Washington, and she started working at a business that made charcoal filters. She got injured at work, and the Department of Labor & Industries (L & I) came into the picture. We didn't have the money to have the surgery done on her hand, so we made an L & I claim. Tammy wanted to quit after that. I wrote the letter to her boss, saying she was giving two months' notice. The boss took several days before answering the letter, and finally said she could get a raise and buy the business!

MARRIED

We decided to buy the filter business, and after a year, we got married. We had felt married for the thirteen years we'd been together. But getting married was supposed to help with taxes. It didn't. I was working with the charcoal without a mask, because I'm claustrophobic. I assumed I would die early anyway from the fumes, so we paid social security taxes for her but not for me. The extra money gave us enough to live on.

We lived in a house behind the factory while she was working in the filter business. I started traveling four days a week, doing other sales to give us more income. We paid off the business in six years instead of seven. But when I was away four days out of every week, Tammy got lonely, and she connected with a guy we both knew.

When I'd call at night, I didn't always reach her. After a while, I asked her what was going on, and she didn't say anything. I completely fixed up her car while she was away, and when she got back, I said, "I'll give you the keys if you'll tell me why we aren't together anymore." When she didn't answer, I slapped her on one side of her face, knocking her over. I knew by then that we were done.

Barb: What did she do then?

Jim: She got a restraining order against me. But we were talking to each other, even while the order was going on. I picked up a lot of things in my travels, working along with two women I knew, who were trying to get off their meth addiction. When I counted up everything I'd purchased, it was *eighteen thousand dollars*! I figured the only way to sell all this stuff was to open a store, so I did that while Tammy was gone. Then I started staying in the store, along with Amanda, a woman my daughter's age, and her mother.

I had a couple of seizures when I was in the store, and I told Amanda not to call 911. "If I die, I die." A friend named Mike from many years ago came to see me, and he said to me, "Jim, you look like *shit*. What time do you want me here tomorrow?" He wasn't asking. He was saying, "You need help." Mike could see it. [Jim's eyes fill up as he talks about this.]

TSUNAMI OF THE MIND

Mike and his daughter-in-law started helping at the store and bringing me food. She got me a library card and the paperwork for me to get food stamps, and the two of them set up a phone for me to use. I had another seizure when I was in the back of the store. Mike thought it was a diabetic coma, so he called Tammy for help, since Tammy's father had diabetes.

I don't know how long it was before I was conscious, but I know I thought I was dead. I actually *hoped* I was dead. Then I saw my ex-wife's face in front of me, and she was crying. All I could think of was, "There are no tears in heaven!" I've always said to people, "I'm okay," whether I am or not. So at that point I tried to stand up a bunch of times, to show I could do it. Finally I was able to stand up, with the help of, of all people, Tammy's boyfriend!

Three days later, after I gotten some help, I knew that my relationship with Tammy was completely over. But for the first time in my life, I didn't want to fight. I had to throw away the hate. I was out of medicine, and I needed to get more. I didn't like Tammy's boyfriend, but when he came to give me a ride to get medicine, I decided to accept what he said. She had a restraining order against me, but we talked to each other, and we managed to make things better.

I know now that I had a good support group then, but I didn't know it at the time.

The secondhand store wasn't making it, so I decided to do an auction to get rid of things. The advertising didn't reach the town where the auction was, so it was a flop. I moved to La Grande, where there was a lot of meth, and I dabbled in meth for several weeks while doing a lot of drinking.

Then I went homeless for a couple of weeks. When it rained hard, I would go into a laundry. When Tammy learned that I was sleeping under a bush behind Safeway, she said, "Why don't you stay at the shop I have?" She twisted my arm, so I got a U Haul. She also asked me if I was taking my anti-seizure medicine. Then the cops said I couldn't keep a trailer next to the business, so she found a trailer park around the corner from her place. "I'll pay the rent," she said, "and you come over and make the filters." I lived there and took the medicine for six months, between November and May. Then I moved over to Vancouver WA, where my brother had lived.

Barb: Did you stop the medicine because of the seizures?

Jim: I don't like medicines in general, and I still have a hard time taking pills. When it's not going my way, I just throw it away. But when I got to Vancouver, I got free medical insurance for the first time, so I went to a doctor. When I was in the hospital in Walla Walla, I had been told I suffer from depression, hepatitis C, and my liver's shot. The sonogram of my liver showed something that looked like cancer. When I heard about that I never went back to that doctor. I don't need to know if I've got cancer or not!

Barb laughs.

Jim: After I got the insurance in Vancouver, I had already filed for Social Security, and Social Security sent me to a psychiatric somebody. That person said there was absolutely nothing wrong with me. My heart's fine, my blood pressure's good, and the brain doctor said there is nothing wrong upstairs.

Barb: So that was better news than the other time.

Jim: Yes. It wasn't feasible to sign a new lease on the apartment in Vancouver, so I found a travel trailer for sale on Craigslist, borrowed the money from Tammy to buy it, and moved here to Long Beach. The doctor down here said I do have hepatitis C, high blood pressure, and the liver seems to be healing itself.

Once I was here, I had a place to stay, but I was sick and tired of being alive. I went over to the DSHS (Dept. of Social and Human Services) office and told them I was having some trouble upstairs. They said that just down the street is the behavioral center. At first I just went past the building, but finally I went in and talked with the person you see if you're thinking of killing yourself. She talked me down and got me an appointment with a counselor. She said, "I don't think you have depression. I think you have bipolar 2." That led me to get some medicine that has finally helped, along with going to classes to deal with my drinking.

I know what I've got to do to get through the program, like stopping the marijuana while I'm in the classes. I've had shoulder pain for a long time, and the marijuana helped with the pain. But my prescribing person found an older antidepressant that is excellent for pain. And once I have my neck operated on, my shoulder won't hurt and I can stay off all the bad drugs.

Barb: Jim, I can see that you've been pushed around a lot in your life! It makes sense that you don't want to be pushed around now. Different people have had different ideas about what's going on in you, but it sounds like the term Bipolar 2 doesn't bother you very much. Does it help you to understand something of how your brain has been operating?

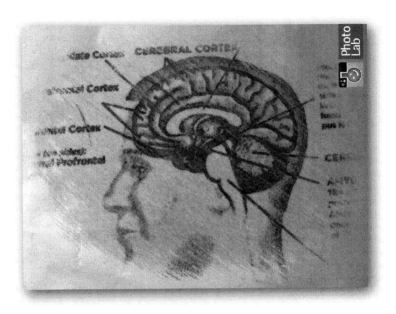

Jim: Yes. It helps me to know that there's something going on in my brain that's not quite right. And with some work, it may not be able to be fixed, but I can learn to live with it better. A lot of it is being able to understand. When I go online and check my thought process, I get an idea of why I think that way, my aggression, and other weird stuff. It's nice to know that there's something wrong upstairs.

If I had known there was something wrong with me, I wouldn't have a daughter; I wouldn't have a son. I would not allow myself to have children when I'm suffering with something, but I had no idea. So I wish when I was born that I would have automatically known, so I could have dealt with it from day one, rather than to wait until I'm in my fifties to start dealing with it.

When I went to prison, people told me I should tell them I was drunk. I wondered, "What do you mean, tell them I was drunk?" They said I might get off easier.

Barb: In a way our whole culture says that. Alcohol is okay, but 'mental health issues' are not.

Jim: I *did* those things that put me in jail! I may not be proud of everything I did, but I'll sure take the rap for it. In fact, I'll even take the rap for something I didn't do. I'm into helping people. I don't mind being homeless. If I can help somebody else not be homeless, I'd do it. There are too many homes that are vacant. For every homeless person there are two houses that are vacant. That's wrong!

My alcohol trainer and I didn't hit it off well at the start, but he listened to me. He went beyond the usual practice, to work along with my mental health counselor. Now the two things are working together instead of in opposite directions.

Barb: Some time ago you said that you resented being born, and recently you told me that you didn't expect to live into your fifties. What do you think about your life now?

Jim: I used to think I'd be dead before now. But now I think I'll live to be ninety-nine, and on my ninety-ninth birthday I'll be at an AA meeting!

Barb: What a great thought! Thanks, Jim.

STEVE

Get out and do something, even though you want to run off and hide. You've got to keep at it. It will get better. It always does.   - Steve

I MET STEVE at a local support group in 2005. We had our first interview in 2007 for a regional mental health newsletter. We met again after Steve moved to Astoria, Oregon. This conversation took place in 2014.

Barb: In our earlier conversation you said that you grew up in Astoria as one of eight children. What were your parents' backgrounds?

PARENTS

Steve: My dad is Swedish and my mom is German. My dad was noticeably moody. He could be jolly at times and grouchy at others. He didn't beat us, but I remember he did slap me one time. A long time later I thought, "Boy, I got my dad's moods." I guess that's common with Scandinavian families.

Barb: I'm curious about how the Scandinavian backgrounds might have affected people. They would live with very long nights for part of the year and very long days for other parts of the year. I don't know any proof of that as a factor in mood illnesses, but it's interesting to consider.

Steve: Yes. I don't know how anyone could survive all that. It would raise hell for somebody trying to deal with the times when you had 24 hours of darkness, and other times when you had 24 hours of light.

Barb: What was life like when you were growing up near the Oregon coast?

Steve: I was a pretty happy kid and pretty upbeat, though I didn't especially enjoy high school. I did well in community college, and I thought I might become a teacher. But that was during the Vietnam War. I heard that maritime service could meet my service obligation, so I decided to go to Baltimore for merchant marine school. I finished that school in 1970 and started working on ships as an engineering officer. Then when I was about 28, I started to experience this feeling of doom and gloom. I knew that was not normal!

DOOM AND GLOOM

I was in the middle of a relationship with the woman who became my wife. At first I thought the gloomy feelings were because of her, and then because of my job going to sea. So I quit going to sea for a while and worked in the shipyard. I tried to figure out what the hell was going on, but I had no clue! I would think too much and not be able to decide what to do. I can remember having times when my mind was raging, for no reason at all.

Somehow I got through that particular time, and we got married in 1976. I started going to college when I wasn't going to sea, thinking I'd get my teaching degree. Things went well for quite some time. We had a child, life was good, and we were enjoying ourselves. So when I was feeling good, I didn't believe that the bad times could happen to me again. It wasn't logical!

When I was 34, I had another episode. Things got really miserable. It was so bad that I said to myself, "I'd better quit going to sea. That must be it." So I took a job in a hospital working as a maintenance engineer. For many years after that I would have recurring depressions once or twice a year that would last up to a month. I would work while depressed, and sometimes I'd hide from other people. I felt anxious and depressed at the same time, even when I was trying different antidepressants. I finally took an overdose of something that wouldn't have killed me anyway, Zanax.

Barb: Do you think the overdose was from trying to get rid of your painful feelings?

Steve: Yes, it was. After that I realized I needed to do something different in order to feel better. So I went into a support group, got a different medication, and things went along okay for a while. I think now that the turning point was five or six years after I had started taking antidepressants. A friend told me about a 12-step support group, Emotions Anonymous, and someone in that group said, "Maybe you should try lithium. I've read a book about it, and it's supposed to be really good!"

I started taking lithium, and it worked. I had no side effects from it, but it was a pain in the ass to have my blood checked every six months. I had been working in the hospital for quite some time and having a good steady routine. I was feeling a lot better, and things seemed to be normal. So I thought, "I want to go back to sea, so I can finish out my pension. It's exciting to be on the ship and there's big money out there." My wife was okay with it, so I went back to sea in 1999.

AT SEA AGAIN

From 1999 to 2001 I worked on ferries between Seattle and Alaska, two weeks on and two weeks off. That went pretty well. I had some ups and downs, but nothing severe. I wanted to go back onto the big ships, so we went to Hawaii, and I worked there from December 2001 to June 2006.

While in Hawaii I was feeling really good working on the ship, and I was bothered by the six month required blood test. So I thought, "I'll just stop taking the lithium and take an antidepressant instead." That was *fine*, until I really hit bottom. I got off the ship and had a lot of free time, and I started to feel _really bad_! That culminated in another suicide attempt. This time it was an overdose of lithium, of all things, which damn near killed me.

Barb: Did that suicide attempt happen in Hawaii?

Steve: Yes. After we had moved to Hawaii I was having so much fun [laughs] and enjoying myself that I decided I didn't need the lithium. I was _so wrong_! I'm damn sure I won't take a chance and try to go off it again. I don't notice it really affecting my moods now, but I' m pretty certain I need it. When I was in the middle of that worst depression, I wasn't thinking at all about my wife and daughter. I just couldn't stand all those raging feelings and thoughts!

We had a home on the Washington coast at the same time we were living in Hawaii. So after we came back from Hawaii I went to a hospital in Portland to have electroconvulsive therapy treatments, or ECT. I was looking for something that might cure me. Every time I had the ECT, I would feel good for about six weeks, and then I'd feel as if I was right back where I started.

Barb: How close together were the electroconvulsive therapy treatments?

Steve: I had three a week. I would feel wonderful for three or four weeks, and then I would start right back again not feeling good. I would just want to go to bed and stay there. I had a total of nine sessions, and I had the same experience each time. After feeling good for a time, I would want to go to bed and just stay there. I think electroconvulsive therapy helps some people, but for me it didn't work in the long run.

What finally got me back into a normal life was making the decision that going to sea wasn't working for me. It was especially hard to experience the up and down moods during the times I was off the ship. On ship I had structured demands, being on watch, sleeping, and eating. I would have that routine for three to six months, and then I would be off the ship for six months. Without the shipboard routine, I couldn't make my own structure and stay on balance emotionally. I see now that a person with a mood disturbance needs routine and a purpose.

In 2006 I quit going to sea permanently. The next year I started working at a regular job. I worked at a local car lot for two years, then at the local museum for another two and a half years. When I had a problem with my boss at the museum, I lost that job. I knew immediately that I'd better get involved with other things so I could keep having a structure for my daily life.

Barb: What kinds of things did you find to do?

VOLUNTEERING

Steve: I started volunteering at the Senior Center, and at the senior meal site. I also joined the boards of two local nonprofits. At first I was washing dishes for Loaves and Fishes, and then they asked me to be on their board. Dishwashing isn't my favorite thing, but it's something that needs to be done and it gave me something regular to do.

One thing I have found out is that I need to forgive myself when I'm doing the volunteer jobs, because I can't always do the best I want to do. I can be harder on myself than anyone else is. You can see from my Mood Tracker[25] [he shows me a graph on paper], that I still have ups and downs! They are not severe, though. I think the lithium keeps me from getting severely depressed.

Barb: I recall that you said earlier about being at sea, that when it was good it was *really good*. Hearing you say that, it makes me wonder whether you found yourself going a little higher than usual at those times. Is that how you remember it?

Steve: Possibly, but I don't generally have the experience of being really high. I don't tend to have hypomania or mania. One good thing about the Mood Tracker is that you can mark down whatever emotional level you are aware of on a given day. The Mood Tracker scale gives you a baseline, so you can mark it as Mildly Elevated, Moderately, or Severely. The range is the same in the other direction - - Mildly Depressed, Moderately, and Severely.

In *three years* I have had only a few mildly elevated days. Using the Mood Tracker lets me tell myself and my doctor what's going on with me from day to day. In my case the lower moods are more frequent. When I'm feeling good I think to myself, "Wow, this is just normal. I feel really good!" I can tell when I'm getting More Elevated, but I've never had anything radical in that direction.

I've had several psychiatrists over the years. One of them told me that the wife of one of his patients had said to him, "You know how Bill is. He's usually a very thrifty, practical guy." The doctor answered, "Yeah, I know, he's always complaining about my fees." But one time she told the doctor, "This week he bought a condo and two brand new cars." That man hadn't had an episode for 25 years!

Barb: That's not like you, apparently. It sounds as if your mood almost never gets elevated to that large a degree.

Steve: No, it's never gotten extreme. But one of my friends is like that man was. She only had two episodes of mania, but when they were mania they were *really mania*! So I know that it can happen. My friend says she almost wishes she had it, because she's musical. When she was in the high mood she was writing music and playing around a great deal. But she says it always ends up being bad.

Barb: From what you've said, you haven't wanted to get rid of the lithium, except for the one time when you were in Hawaii. Is that right?

Steve: No, I haven't felt that way any time since then. That time was a matter of inexperience with lithium. I couldn't tell if I really needed it or not! I've found that to be true of other medicines too. You don't know that it's helping you until you stop taking it. With my allergy pills, I forgot to take them for a week and didn't fill up my pill container. All of a sudden I said to myself, "Why are my allergies so terrible?"

EMOTIONS ANONYMOUS[26]

Barb: Earlier you mentioned an Emotions Anonymous group. Where did you find that group?

Steve: We were living in Vancouver, and the group was across the river in Tigard. My friend had started the group. She and I have been friends now for many years, ever since the time I had that suicide attempt in 1986. The two of us have stayed in communication all this time. She has a problem that they now call Bipolar Type 2, where you never get the mania. In her case, her mood doesn't come up to baseline very often. That really sucks.

Barb: I've been living with Bipolar 2 myself.

Steve: Really?

Barb: But my happier times sound as if they are more enjoyable than in your friend's case. I'm active in a variety of ways that help structure my days and connect me with other people. But I have never bought two cars or done some of the other wild things you described!

For a number of years I've been reading about the different forms of bipolar disorder. There are some indications that bipolar 2, bipolar depression, is significantly more widespread than manic depression or bipolar one. Unfortunately, that fact is not known or understood by many primary care doctors. So a person with mood cycles may come to the doctor with symptoms of depression. If the doctor doesn't know the individual's history and doesn't have time to dig deeper, the result may be simply a prescription for an antidepressant. As you've seen in your own life, that can lead to problems. The more knowledge we have, the better it is for us.

TRACKING MOODS

Steve: My current doctor says he loves my Mood Tracker. He's often said to me, "I want you to make a tape, so I could show my other patients. I wish other people would use it." I can see why he would like other people to use it. Many people don't often get to see their psychiatrist, so it can be hard to know how a person is doing between doctor's visits.

In my situation the psychiatrist sees me only every six months. The Mood Tracker gives my primary care doctor a record of what is happening in terms of cycles. It also keeps track of my sleep. My own sleep pattern is up and down like a yoyo. I sleep okay, but sometimes I'll bang out ten hours, and once in a great while I'll drop down to six or seven [showing the graph]. The green line here is the daily sleep pattern. This other line is the mood.

Barb: So you are writing this down every day.

Steve: Yes. I log it into the computer on MoodTracker.com. And it's free! They have a deluxe version that you pay a little bit more for. I don't know what the difference is, so I've always used the standard one. It's such a blessing. If I thought they were going out of business I'd start paying! It also serves as a good diary for me.

Barb: As you look at this mood line and the sleep patterns, how much sleep is a regular amount for you?

Steve: It varies, but it can be nine or ten or more when I include naps, That one went up to 11 or 12 [pointing at the graph], but I didn't report it as a day I was depressed. You can see that on some days I'm inclined to sleep more when I've got this valley, a mild depression.

Barb: Ah – more sleep may mean more depression.

Steve: I'm not certain which of them comes first. If you're feeling down you'd rather not go out and do things. One great thing about having the Mood Tracker over the past several years is that it gives me the confidence to know that this too shall pass. I can look back and say to myself, "I got over it then, and I will again." What it also shows me is that every couple or three months I'm going to have a spell. It's not horrible; it's just not feeling my normal optimistic self.

Barb: That makes sense. And when you think about a time when you wanted to be doing a lot, or doing nothing, can you come back and look at it and say, "Ah –that was it" when this happens?

Steve: Sure. I recognize, and I imagine you do too, times when you feel like crying, don't have any optimism, or feel like "What's the use?" It's not bad enough that you go to bed and cover up your head, but sometimes you'd love to! You're in a group and you want to go off by yourself. That's not normal for me, but I realize now that it's part of normality.

Barb: Yes. So you're telling me that these days you keep busy doing quite a few different things – driving people in town, washing dishes, volunteering at the senior center, and other things. On the days when you're feeling a little lower than average, how do you take care of yourself?

Steve: I just keep going. Just keep going. Sometimes you don't feel like it and you just keep going. I'm sure you know about that.

Barb: Yes. That reminds me of the saying, "Fake it until you make it."

Steve: That's right. Stay with it until you start to feel better. I admit that it makes me mad at times when I know I should be enjoying myself, and I'm not. When I'm really depressed, I'm convinced that this is just the way it is. I'm thinking, "Things are really bad, people are all a bunch of jerks, and it's hopeless." When I listen to myself saying those things now, I stop, and then I realize that those thoughts are not true!

Barb: Yes. By the way, how long have you and Doris been married?

Steve: Thirty-eight years. Wow! She has had some mood swings too. She hasn't had good luck with antidepressants, but her experiences have been within a range that she's been able to cope with. Others in our family have had those issues too. Sometimes I've been able to talk with some of them about my experience.

I worked with a guy who was up and wired some days, and other days he'd be really grouchy and grumpy. I don't know this for sure, but I would guess that he might have mood issues but would not try to get help. He's always said it was the other people fouling up! It occurs to me that a lot of people may be functional but dealing with bipolar issues. Maybe it's not nearly as rare as people say.

Barb: That's a major reason that I decided to have these conversations. After knowing you and others for a number of years, I realized that there are quite a few people who are interested, and even eager, to talk with me about their hard times and how they've gotten through them. I feel sure, Steve, that your story will be encouraging to other people who feel isolated and alone. I imagine many of them are saying to themselves, "Nobody else is *as bad*, or as *worthless*, or as *stuck*, as I am."

Steve: Exactly. And I'm sure there's a high percentage of people who just won't go for help. The only times I would agree to get help, it had gotten so bad that I absolutely *couldn't stand* it anymore! I used to get agitated depression. I don't know if you have that, and fortunately I don't seem to get it anymore, but it was just *horrible*. It would have to be that bad, that impossible to deal with, for me to go ahead and seek help. But when it's not that bad, I just bump along.

Barb: I have experienced agitated depression at times too. I wonder though, about the question of being willing to seek help. Do you think men more than women resist the idea of asking for help? I think of my father and two brothers, as well as other men I've known. I can hear almost all of them saying, especially to their boys, "Be a Man!" - - and often along with it, "Don't be a *girl!*"

Steve: Actually I had my sister to talk with about it, because she'd gone through her own tough periods too. Actually I think two of my sisters had mood problems. I thought that theirs were not as severe as mine. But that may be because I was a man, and when it got really bad I thought, "This is it. I'm checking out!" [He laughs.]

Barb: Thank goodness you didn't check out when you felt like doing it!

As you think now, Steve, about what's helped you get to a more positive place in life, what other thoughts do you have that you'd want to share with somebody else who's feeling kind of "*Ynneehh*, I'm a mess, I can't do anything?!"

Steve: The big thing for me is to say to myself, "This too shall pass. Keep going, and keep doing what you're doing, providing it is something good." If you're just sitting around in your room, in front of a computer or the TV, that's not good. Get out, and when you're having a hard time, fake it until you make it.

That's what a psychiatrist told me one time when I was in a psych ward. Both times I tried to off myself, I ended up in a psych ward. When the psychiatrist came in, I said to him, "You guys are just trying to keep me alive. The only reason you try to keep me alive is so you can get all my money!" I was concerned about my insurance at that point, and the amount of money I had left for retirement. The doctor said, "Believe me, I've been a psychiatrist for twenty-five years. Anxious people stay anxious. Depressed people always get over it!"

Barb: That's interesting.

Steve: At least that was his take on it. I think he was trying to convince me, that just because I was depressed now, it wouldn't last forever. I would get over it.

Barb: And in your case, he was right!

Steve: I believe that not too many depressed people stay depressed their entire lives. That would be very hard.

Barb: Yes. Again, from the reading I've been doing, I understand that there are fewer people overall who have what's called unipolar depression – depression that continues throughout a person's life. Significantly more people have depression symptoms some of the time but also have the ups and downs. For me personally, when I'm in the middle of a down time I don't believe that there's an up time coming soon. When you're in it, the feeling is, "*T h i s   i s   t h e   h o l e !*"

Steve: Yeah. I remember that feeling that you're going to cry, and thinking that for sure you're not going to get over this one. "This one's going to be different. I'm never going to get over this one."

Barb: That's really true! [Laughs]

Steve: I can laugh about it now when I am feeling fine, but it's not so funny when you're in it. I remember that I used to go to the NAMI meetings when I lived nearby, but sometimes I was too depressed to go.

Barb: You're not alone in that. When I was feeling down but having to chair a NAMI meeting, it was not fun at all! The more you and I talk, the more I can see the real power of using the Mood Tracker over a period of time. Did you hear about it from a psychiatrist or find it on your own?

Steve: I heard about it from my local psychiatrist. He's a good guy. I had to stop seeing him because he didn't take Medicare. He's the one who thought that I could make a tape so he could try to convince some of his other patients to try the Mood Tracker. I actually have tried talking with other people about the Mood Tracker, but I guess people are hesitant to try something new.

Barb: I've seen that about other things I've mentioned to people. I don't know if the stories of the ten people in *Tsunami of the Mind* are going to change everyone's mind either. But it's been interesting for me to hear what people say when I say the title of the book. I mention what it is about, and most of the responses are, "I want to read that book!" That feels good.

REGULAR PEOPLE

I believe many people want to get a sense of regular people's lives, including their struggles. Fortunately not as many people say these days that you're either *crazy* or *normal,* with nothing in between. There's more openness and curiosity now about what goes on inside each of us. On the other hand, using terms like mental health *versus* physical health can be a problem. What I call tsunamis of the mind really <u>do</u> happen in the brain!

Steve: I know this book project is part of your journey. You have wanted to do this for a number of years. I remember our first conversation in 2007 that became a newsletter article. Wasn't the article called "An Engineer with Emotions?" It was good for me to tell you about the Emotions Anonymous group. The group really helped me, and it led to friendships that I wouldn't have had otherwise. I even thought of starting one of those groups myself.

Barb: I remember our first conversation too. You got me started thinking about the power of individual stories. And I was really interested in your working on boilers, on ships and in hospitals. It sounded like hard work, and it was nothing I had ever known about.

Steve: It was hard work, at least some of the time, and I liked that about it. When I had a regular routine on the ship I had specific things to do at certain times. When you're doing that work, or any regular work, it's easy. You work, you get off work, you're tired, you go home, you watch TV, and you go to bed. It was always best for me to be busy busy busy. These days as a volunteer my work is to do things with people who need my help, and that's good.

It may sound strange, but sometimes I think it can help to be depressed! When I've been in a somewhat lower mood, it got me to do some things that I needed to do, things I might not have done otherwise. I knew I had to stay active, and being responsible to do things like driving people places could put me in a more positive frame of mind.

Barb: I can see that.

Steve: My current routine is a much better arrangement than when I was working at the museum. It's much more rewarding. My days are a little scattered sometimes, but - -

Barb: But more fun than not?

Steve: For sure. I love these people. They are really nice people.

Barb: I think that's a key for folks like us, to be around people who want to connect with us.

Steve: Right. I think it's a personality thing too. Some people may not feel the way we do. They may be happy staying more by themselves. I have one friend is married to a guy who is happiest when he's working in his shop. He finally quit drinking, which had been *bad,* so now his days are spent by himself in the shop. Some people don't like to be around people, and you've got to accept that too - - as long as it's a not a matter of staying away from people just because you're depressed.

Barb: Right.

Steve: I think everybody needs some exposure to other people, at least some of the time.

Barb: Yes. When I get involved with somebody else, my attention and my thoughts go to them. That way my feelings are less centered on myself and how well or badly I am doing at the moment. When I really *see* that other person, that person matters as much as me. You know, researchers have found that the brain has mirror neurons, brain cells that are active when we pay attention to what someone else is doing. When I heard about mirror neurons, I thought about how I like accompanying singers on the piano. I like accompanying much more than playing solos, because I can focus on *them* rather than myself. My brain knows what makes me happier!

At this point in our lives, it's especially important for us to be connecting back and forth with each other. Many years ago, when I spent a summer in southern Africa, I heard the African word that conveys what I think we both are saying, about community. It is *Ubuntu - - I am, because we are.*

Steve: Yeah. I get that.

And now [he gestures to the hallway] I guess I should get going. The group is waiting for me.

Barb: Thanks again, Steve, for taking time to talk. Enjoy the group!

CAROL

After I left the forum on Altered States and Suicide I thought, "I don't have to hide any more. I'm not alone."   - Carol

CAROL AND *I met when I visited her Alternatives to Suicide Peer Support group in western Massachusetts. I learned about these groups through a mental health webinar. We met at Carol's apartment in the fall of 2014.*

Barb: Thanks for letting me come visit you, Carol. Before the tape started, you said you grew up as the youngest of four children.

Carol: We were all five years apart. My dad was a mechanic at a Ford dealership, and my mom stayed at home with us. My grandfather had a cottage on a lake, and we spent our summers there. When my mother inherited money from her uncle, my parents built a permanent house at the lake. We lived there year-round after I was in fourth grade.

EARLY YEARS

Barb: Did you spend a lot of time in the water?

Carol: I did when I was very young. But I had ear infections and was constantly breaking my eardrums, which led to a mastoid problem. After my first ear surgery I was told not to get any water in my ears. I think my mother understood how hard that was for me, so she paid for me to take horseback riding lessons, and later the Famous Artists School course. She knew I needed to have other things to do.

My grandmother lived with us, so when my parents would go out on Friday nights, Grandma made special desserts and played house with me. She was also a wonderful gardener, and the first craftsperson in my life. I would go with her to her local sewing circle, so I got to know a lot of older people.

Before we moved to the lake I spent my Saturdays at the movie theatre in town. Movies and coloring were my major entertainment. My dad's shirt cardboards had pictures printed on them, and I colored those too.

Barb: You said at the start that your parents were encouraged not to think of you as hearing-impaired, although you couldn't hear well.

Carol: That's right. Things sounded funny on one side versus the other side, and I would say "What?" all the time. I would finish people's sentences with what I thought they were saying. Often that wasn't what they said, so my family adjusted by just repeating their words. I didn't know I was deaf, so I didn't feel any stigma about being deaf. I didn't know I was missing anything.

I had my tonsils and adenoids taken out when I was 5 years old. That was a major trauma. I was the last of four kids to go into the operating room. I saw each of the others come back after their surgeries, and they didn't look good. It scared me. They gave me a sedative, which was my first paradoxical reaction to medication. I also reacted to the ether anesthetic. I had my first out-of-body experience; my mind just went somewhere else. My mother said I nearly died. I don't remember anything after the surgery. It affected me for years afterwards.

Barb: That must have been really scary, especially when you couldn't hear well. When you started school, what was that like for you?

Carol: I remember I lost a tooth on the school stairs when I was in kindergarten. Then in second grade I was terrified at being kept inside as punishment for something I did or didn't do. I needed to pee, but I was too scared to go to the bathroom and I peed in the waste basket in the classroom.

I missed a lot of primary school because of constant ear infections, and I often didn't hear the teacher's directions in class. Finally my mother took me for a hearing test, and then to see an ear specialist. That happened when I was going into the fourth grade.

Barb: You mentioned going to the movies. Did you enjoy the visuals and colors?

Carol: Oh yes! Walt Disney's "Fantasia" was the best thing ever. The colors and motions went with the sound, and different instruments were in different colors. I loved it! I had no idea how much information I was missing in regular movies and on television until years later, when they began to offer captions.

My family didn't do a lot with doctors. But once when I was little I had to go to a doctor for a booster shot, and I wanted no part of it! The doctor slapped me and said some words I don't remember. I don't remember the shot, so I may have disassociated. My parents bribed me to get me to see the ear specialist, because another doctor had hurt me. I refused to go. Their bribe was butterscotch sundaes, so that may have contributed to my using food to comfort myself.

BARBARA BATE, PHD

HEARING AND ART

I had my first ear surgery in 1964, when I was in fourth grade and we were living at the lake. I didn't have much fear about the ear surgery, which amazes me because of my earlier experiences. I got a tutor for a few months to help with my study skills. That's where I learned how to use a dictionary, which was the best thing in the world!

In my early years and all through my teens, I spent a lot of time making art. I colored, doodled, taught myself to paint, crochet, and make earrings. I was in my mid-teens when my mom bought me the Famous Artists School Course, and that opened new doors of possibilities

I made a friend in junior high who is still my best friend 40+ years later. We were both slightly chunky and didn't like gym, but we definitely liked art. Our eighth grade art teacher had us do all kinds of things during art class, and I just loved her. I was one of her best students, and I got an A.

In ninth grade I had to change schools, so my friend and I were separated. The kids made fun of me that year. I suspect now that my responses made them laugh because I was only hearing out of one ear.

My ninth grade art teacher was fantastic. She had us make a color chart, tints from light to dark, so I became good at mixing and matching colors. She was the one who recommended me to the drama department. I was able to match colors and finish the scenery for a school play, after they'd had trouble getting the colors right. That was one of my proudest memories in ninth grade.

Barb: So the teacher noticed you were good at those things.

Carol: Yes. For the rest of high school my friend and I were back in the same school, and we started an art club. We entered a design contest at the local Volkswagen dealer, painting a Volkswagen Beetle with a Persian rug design so it looked like a magic carpet. We won first prize! [She laughs.] That was my fondest memory in eleventh grade. We used the prize money to buy things for the art club. We made enameled art palette pins for all the members.

Barb: That was a perfect symbol for your group.

Carol: Yes, it was! Eleventh grade was a really fun year. I didn't take art my senior year, so there was a gap until I started to draw with an ink pen in college.

Barb: Apart from art classes, what was high school like for you?

Carol: I took home economics class, grooming me to be a woman who stayed home and raised kids. But I didn't fit into that mold. The women's movement had started when I graduated in 1971. I had been raised with the traditional views about women, but when I was exposed to other ideas it messed me up for a while.

Barb: What was said in your family about male-female relationships and sex?

Carol: My mom told me absolutely nothing about sex. Neither did my older sister, except by scaring me once with a comment she made. I was asked to go out with the brother of my sister's girlfriend. He was a soldier home on leave from Vietnam. When I got home from the date, my sister said, "Nice boys don't give hickeys." I thought, "What is she talking about?" I walked into the bathroom and saw this blood-sucking thing on my neck. I thought, "Oh My God, I'm pregnant!" I obviously knew nothing about pregnancy! My date didn't take advantage of me, but he could have. I was lucky.

Barb: What happened when you finished high school?

Carol: I didn't know what to do. People like my older brother and sister got married right after high school. My other brother went to college, but girls in my family didn't. The few friends I had were going away to college. I remember getting seriously depressed for the first time then, but I didn't have anyone to talk with about it.

My mother paid for me to go to the local community college, and I moved out of the house when I started college. My first idea was to be a forest ranger, like the woman who was my twelfth grade biology teacher. But my male adviser said, "Women don't become forest rangers." And I believed him. You don't question authority!

BOSTON TRIP

During my first semester at college, I enjoyed exploring my new-found freedom. Two of the young women I was hanging around with talked about going to New York and Boston. One of them said they had friends we could stay with. So I agreed to drive them from Michigan to New York and Massachusetts. We didn't have much money, so we ran all the tolls from New York to Boston, and picked up a hitchhiker who wrote a check for gas.

When we got to Boston, I found out the so-called friends we were to stay with didn't exist. I had gone along with them all that way, and suddenly it was just too much! I exploded with anger. I stopped the car in the middle of Massachusetts Avenue, and I started a fight with one of the women. The next thing I knew we were surrounded by cops and hauled off to jail. They took my car away.

Barb: When you look back, would you say that was kind of manic?

Carol: It was very impulsive. I didn't know anything about manic behavior at that point. But after being depressed at the end of high school and then being exposed to the wider world, I thought, "Well, I will do the things *I* want to do." Looking back on it now, I realize I was doing things I never thought I would do in my life.

CHARLIE AND IAN

The night we got arrested was the night I met Charlie [laughs]. The judge threw our case out of court, and basically told us to go home. Charlie and I started seeing each other in Boston, and when I went home to Michigan he hitchhiked there to see me. I became pregnant in Michigan, still not knowing anything about birth control. We got married in Michigan and then came back to Massachusetts.

Our son Ian was born in Arlington, Massachusetts. When he was 6 months old we moved to western Massachusetts. We rented a trailer. When things started not working with Charlie, we separated and I moved into an apartment with my son. Then Charlie and I divorced, and I had my next big depression.

After Charlie and I separated I had my second ear surgery. It was ten years after my first mastoid surgery. I was in the middle of a deep depression, which led to my spending three weeks in a psychiatric unit, for the first time.

PHIL

While I was in the hospital I met Phil, who was also a patient there. After both of us were released, we started seeing each other. I had grown up around parties and alcohol, but with Phil I learned how it was to be with a full-blown alcoholic. Phil would come home from work, have a six-pack of beer, and be passed out by eight o'clock. A year into our relationship I started going to Al-Anon, where I learned to stop aiding and abetting. After many rounds of detox, Phil was getting sicker and sicker, but with the help of Al-Anon I was getting healthier.

Barb: How did things go with your son Ian and Phil?

Carol: Ian was 3 or 4 years old when Phil and I got together. Phil played the stepdaddy role, and they did things like going fishing together. But Phil and I often argued after Ian had gone to bed, and I know Ian heard some of it. We didn't hit each other, but we got pretty angry.

One particular night Phil went out with a neighbor and was drinking hard liquor. When he came home, it got really bad, and he hit me. Then he destroyed our bedroom, so I called the police. When they got there, he was sitting in the living room as if nothing had happened. I said to the police, "I'm not pressing charges, but he's not staying here." They escorted him out of the house, and he stayed at his buddy's home.

In the morning Phil came back and wanted to get into the house. I said, "No, You can't come in. Look through the window and see what you did." He was having blackouts at that point, and they teach you in Al-Anon not to cover up the consequences, so I had left the bedroom as it was the night before. I gave him some clothes while the police were there, since I didn't want him coming into the house after they had left.

A week after the incident, Phil came and told me he was on his way to Greenfield Detox. He'd had a spiritual awakening, and he didn't want to lose me. I said, "We'll see." And he did get sober.

I remember that when I was in college, I had a girlfriend who was so beat up by her boyfriend that the hospital took photos of her, as evidence to take to court. Then she dropped the charges, and she married this person. Until Phil, I couldn't understand why women kept going back. Now I knew.

Phil was working for a detox facility, and in his second year of sobriety I got pregnant. I had terminated a pregnancy early in our relationship, fearing that if someone drank, there could be something wrong with the child. But this time I was hopeful, and I had vowed never again to go through an abortion.

PREGNANCY

Barb: How did Phil react to your being pregnant?

Carol: While I was pregnant and he was sober, he seemed really pleased. He was working at the detox facility. But things became strange the closer I got to my due date. I realized later that Phil's drinking had started at a very young age, because of childhood traumas.

When Phil was sober during my pregnancy, he couldn't cover up the emotions from his early abuse, and those feelings started surfacing. Seeing what was happening, Phil's wonderful boss at the detox facility urged him to take leave and sign himself into the Brattleboro Retreat after the baby was born.

Barb: How did the birth go?

Carol: It was a natural childbirth, with Ian and Phil both participating. His coworkers had bought us a stroller, and we seemed to be doing well as a family, as far as I could tell. But then Phil went to the

Brattleboro Retreat, and I went to visit him on a Monday. He was out-doors, and when he saw me he immediately said, "Let's go!" We left, and I didn't get to talk to any of the staff.

Barb: What is the Brattleboro Retreat?

Carol: It is a famous mental health facility in southern Vermont. When Phil got home that day, he was talking crazy. After I put the baby to bed, Phil cried and said he wouldn't come upstairs. He said he was afraid he would hurt me or the baby. We talked about finding some help for him the next morning, and after a while he seemed calmer. Two hours later I got up to feed the baby, and Phil and the car were gone.

PHIL'S SUICIDE

At 6 a.m. I called everyone who might know where he was. A friend told me she'd heard on her scanner a description of a car that matched my car. Then in the afternoon, two cop cars pulled into my lot. They asked me to step inside the house, but I didn't need to; I knew he was gone.

My whole world was turned around. Two days after Phil's death, his elderly grandmother also died, so we had two funerals that week. My mother and sister came from Michigan, and one brother flew in from North Carolina. They stayed for a week, and they did what they could to help. But after they left, I got more and more depressed.

I started seeing a therapist, but that didn't seem to help. Knowing I was getting worse, I asked Carl's godparents if they would take Carl if I needed to go into the hospital. They said they would.

Barb: How old was Ian at that point?

Carol: Ian was 12 years old, and Carl was 3 months old. My friends took Ian with them as well, so they were watching both my kids. The therapist had seen that I was getting more and more despondent, so he had me go directly to the hospital. While I was in the hospital, my friend took Carl with her to the place where she worked, and everybody fell in love with him.

Sometime after I got out of the hospital, that same friend suggested that I might want to think about moving on. That was far from my mind. But my friend mentioned a man she knew, and I agreed to meet him.

DAVID

For our first date, David and I went to the Clark Museum, pushing Carl in the stroller. Looking back, I think David fell in love with my son more than with me. But that was enough reason for me to want to stay alive.

Some months later David hurt himself, and I offered to take care of him – a little like Florence Nightingale. While I was caring for him, he asked me to marry him. When he got better, he almost called off the wedding, but then he changed his mind, and we pulled off a wedding in three days! I told David in no uncertain terms that if things didn't work out with us, he could _not_ abandon my kids. They'd had too much tragedy already.

We had been married for six months when David left. But at that point he just moved down the street. He still saw the kids, played Daddy to Carl and Ian, and was there for the boys for several years until he moved farther away, eventually living in Florida.

Technically I'm still married to David. We laugh and say it's the longest marriage for each of us. Carl is now almost 29. Carl was 15 months old when David and I got married, and Ian was 13. David and I are still friends. We still laugh and hug, but we don't live together. He lives east of here now, in Orange, Massachusetts.

I'm grateful that David's been there for the boys. One time, when they both got into trouble, he called each of them and was supportive of both of their issues. He's continued to be part of their lives. But I decided not to have any more men in my life. Trusting men was too big an issue!

WORK AND ART

Barb: What kind of work were you doing while you were raising the boys?

Carol: I was in school while I was with David. I finished a certificate program in business microcomputers and an associate's degree in liberal arts. Then I kept taking art classes whenever I could, while I was doing other jobs. When I was doing the certificate program, I got interested in computer graphics, along with doing the pen and ink work I'd done before. Ian graduated from high school in 1991, and I think my graduation was in 1992. I had wanted to make sure that our graduations didn't conflict.

Then for three years I worked with an herb company that made dry dip mixes and herbal vinegars. Within a month of being there, I was manager of my section. At one point I had 16 people making herbal vinegar for Marshall's and other stores. I also designed their labels, and I did the art for their catalogs. My fantasy was to move out of the vinegar room and into all design work. Then the boss said he didn't want me to do the design work any longer. I was angry, and I said, "If I didn't need a job so much, I'd quit!" So he terminated me, and I applied for unemployment. It had been a big misunderstanding. I'm not so good expressing myself when I'm upset.

TSUNAMI OF THE MIND

Losing that job was hard. I was making car payments, and I almost lost my car. I was working part-time at Crystal in Shelburne Falls, a New Age music, jewelry, book, and clothing store. When I lost the job at the herb place, I took on more hours at the store.

TRIP OUT WEST

My father had died in the 1980s, when I was living with Phil. He had been in his early sixties, and his death was a total shock. My mother died suddenly as well, in 1998, so I never got to say goodbye to either of my parents.

After Dad died, I started having panic attacks. Going to school was hard, but I still wanted to learn. Later, after my mother died, I took a desktop publishing course, and I used some of my inheritance to cover the cost.

After I finished the desktop publishing course, my kids and I took a two month trip out West that we had planned for some time. I had wanted to do something special with them, and I had some extra money from the inheritance. We left Massachusetts with our camping gear, planning to go across the country, including the Grand Canyon. The first weekend we got to Upper Michigan. Ian sprained his ankle, and at the end of the week Carl broke his leg!

Barb: Oh no! How?

Carol: Carl had jumped off a boat into the water, and his leg snapped. We found out he had a bone cyst, and that's what made the leg snap. We had trouble getting the leg stabilized, tried different casts, and finally got a cast that went from the ankle to the hip. We were staying on an island, so we had to leave the island to go to town for emergency work. Carl had just graduated from sixth grade. His reward was a week at the Wizards of the Coast Game Camp in Seattle during our two months on vacation.

After Carl's accident, we called Seattle to see if they could accommodate him with a broken leg, and they said they could. So we re-routed the trip from upper Michigan across the country and went directly to Seattle for Carl's magic camp. The Grand Canyon was too hot that summer, so the farthest south we went was from San Francisco to Sequoia and Kings Canyon National Parks.

Barb: Where did you and Ian go while Carl was at the camp?

Carol: Ian and I went across to the Olympic Peninsula. On the last day when we were headed to the car ferry, Ian took a fall in the woods. We went to the clinic in the nearest town and they gave him crutches and an air cast. When we picked up Carl in Seattle, both of my sons were on crutches! [Both laugh.]

Barb: You wanted an adventure!

Carol: It was an amazing adventure. I bought a $50 park pass at Glacier National Park. It was the best $50 I ever spent. We went to 23 national parks, rerouting the trip to go to places we wanted to see. Carl wanted to see the agates at one particular beach, so he found a way to climb down a long stairway to get to the beach. I still don't know how he did that!

Despite all the ups and downs it was a great trip. We had moose in our campground when we were in Yosemite, and at Yellowstone, we were there on the 25th of August, the traditional day to celebrate Christmas at Yellowstone Park.

Having to do everything for the boys took a lot out of me. Because of Carl's leg-length cast, we took a motel room once a week so he could have a shower. We camped the rest of the time. It was the most intensely close time the three of us ever had. Carl and Ian both talked about that trip as the highlight of their lives.

JOBS

When I came back from the trip in the fall of 2000, I couldn't find any work in graphics. So I started a business with a close friend, using $10,000 from my inheritance. The timing for our business was off, so we didn't succeed. When the business flopped, my friend was upset about my losing all that money. Our friendship fell apart for a while, but we are connected now. She lives in Missouri. My other best friend lives in Michigan. We can be apart for a long time, and there's no distance whenever we meet.

My next job was driving a special needs school bus for an 11-year-old boy. He had autism and was very big for his age. The first day he got out of the bus, he slammed the door so hard it broke the window. I thought to myself, "What have I gotten myself into?"

I developed sciatic issues from driving, which started me looking for new work. Also during this time, I was tired all the time and falling asleep during the day, so I got tested for sleep apnea. The sleep study showed that I got only 10 minutes of sleep each hour at night. I had severe apnea, requiring me to get a CPAP machine (Continuous Positive Airway Pressure).

After I stopped driving the special education bus, my next job turned out to be my dream job. I had taken an adult education course in library science when Ian was little, so that gave me a chance to become an elementary school librarian. The master's level librarian teacher had just left, and here I was! This new job fit me like a glove. It worked well with my ADD and hyper-focus, as well as my love of books and art and creative projects.

I did all kinds of things to help the kids learn how to read. At one point I was running three book fairs a year, two for the library and a Buy One Get One Free fair for the kids. The book fairs made money so I could buy books for the library, since we had only a small budget for buying books. My eight years at that job became my happiest time ever.

Then it suddenly ended. The school budget committee met when the interim superintendent and the principal, both of whom supported my work, were out of town. I got a phone message from the principal, who was sorry to hear my job had been cut from the budget. I was in shock. It was as if someone had cut my heart out! They had no reason to fire me, and I still needed to work. So I was transferred to work with a special needs student, then as an aide to the rest of the fourth graders. I had to learn the times tables all over again!

I started seeing a therapist, through the school wellness program. I was still distraught over losing the job I loved, but I did start drawing again! After a fifth grade teacher saw me drawing on the bus at a field trip, I was asked to give a presentation to the fifth graders. I also went to art classes with the fourth graders. These experiences helped me to start using art as a stress reliever again.

CAR ACCIDENT

The next September I had a serious car accident on the way home from the school, resulting in head and neck injuries. Again, that changed the dynamic of my life! A month after the accident, I started having constant migraines. I was disoriented, and hearing was also a problem. I couldn't go back to work, and I was desperate for relief. So I was taken for neurological testing. The neurologist suggested a particular antidepressant. He told me, "One of the benefits of this drug, besides helping with your depression, is that it's good for migraines and insomnia."

I took the antidepressant, and it did not help with the migraines, the insomnia, or the depression. I got worse over the next three days, but on the fourth day I felt better. So I thought, "It seems to be working." But the next day I woke up feeling worse than before. After I had my session with my cranial-sacral physical therapist, I went to the neurologist, and I said I didn't feel right. So all he did was to walk me over to the emergency room and drop me off there. I had no idea I was there for psychiatric observation.

This happened on Friday. I was told I needed to sign myself into the hospital for three days of observation. I could leave in three days if everything went well. But they didn't say that the three days would start on Monday! I was working as extra help at the clothing store, so I said to them, "I've got to be out of here by Tuesday." Luckily the doctor could tell on Saturday that I wasn't in the acute state I had been in on Friday.

Barb: Was this the same doctor who had prescribed the earlier antidepressant?

Carol: No. The hospital psychiatrist saw me on the day they admitted me, and then on each of the next three days. On Monday he agreed to let me leave on Tuesday, *if* I agreed to go to the outpatient hospital program. I said I would.

The hospital doctor said I'd had a paradoxical manic reaction to this antidepressant drug. That meant that the medication had acted the opposite way in my body, making my insomnia and headaches worse and making me more depressed.

While I was an outpatient other drugs were tried, none of which helped. So additional psychological testing was ordered. That report said that I had post-concussion disorder, aggravated ADHD, and bipolar illness.

That whole winter was hard. I was staying in respite housing for most of February, and I started asking questions of their medication provider. "You keep giving me antipsychotic or antidepressant drugs, and I keep having one paradoxical reaction after another. I'm an ADHD person. Maybe you should give me an upper, and it will bring me up instead of down." She agreed to try the experiment, and it seemed to help. I didn't feel as depressed or as suicidal as before.

Barb: I also think you had gone through many losses prior to that time. Your brain had been traumatized!

Carol: Yes, it was a crazy time. When I was terminated from my school job, I had applied for both disability and unemployment, not knowing which I was going to get. I received first the disability, then unemployment. The disability payment was reduced while I was collecting unemployment, but I got through the school year with the help of both.

ART SHOW

Then I took six months to write a business plan and apply for grants in support of my art career. The first grant, for my art show, came from the Western Mass Recovery Learning Community's (RLC) Career Initiatives Project. In this book [showing me a large notebook] are one hundred examples of my art that I have done from 1993 to 2013, picked out of over 700 pieces.

I also applied to the Massachusetts Rehabilitation Commission (MRC) for the materials to start my art business. That grant included a high-quality camera, I-Pad, printer-scanner, and various kinds of art materials. Being in a more stable period, I said to myself, "I can finally do it!" Having real money to spend on art supplies felt like "YEAH!"

TSUNAMI OF THE MIND

This past year, I lost two people who meant a lot to me. One was the woman who helped mat all my material for my 100-piece art show. She was a tremendous support. She gave me the use of her studio near here, in Montague MA, while she lived on the coast. After she had a near-death experience of her own, she gave up her studio here. That hit me hard. Then this past winter, my other artist friend, who had been teaching me watercolor painting, suddenly dropped dead. I had seen her in the fall, when she was showing her work at the artist coop gallery in Shelburne Falls. Her death shook me to my core.

When you saw me at the first Alternatives to Suicide support group this past spring (2014), I was in that flux area that's not very comfortable for me. I hadn't spent the rest of the money from the Recovery Learning Community grant to do my art show, or the rest of the grant money for the equipment I wanted for my art studio. So I had a lot of stress, and it felt like a downward spiral.

Barb: It sounds like a time of up and down, up and down.

Carol: Yes. You get to a place and think things are going to stay up. But then I was back to where I was after the car accident. I didn't go quite as far down each time something happened, but it seems like there's always been something coming at me.

Apart from Phil's death, this has been the most trying time of my life. I've become aware that suicide can seem like one way of not having to deal with all these things - - the headaches, my not remembering things, the stresses, and not knowing what to do for the rest of my life.

No one had talked about mental health when I was growing up, so I had no one to talk to when I had my near-death experience and depression at the end of high school. Later on, the idea of suicide became real again when I had the unbelievable migraines. The only thing that helped me with a migraine was to smoke pot. I had no appetite, and I wouldn't eat anything unless I smoked a joint. I couldn't even take Tylenol. There was nothing to relieve that pain!

The doctors wanted me to stop the pot, the cigarettes, everything. So I said, "Fine!" and I stopped the cigarettes and pot. I wanted to see if my life could be different if I wasn't smoking. Then I started taking ADD medicine, which helped, but after a while I was having an allergic reaction to the ADD medicine. So I asked myself, "What am I going to do now?"

FUNCTIONAL MEDICINE

When I realized that the ADD medicine wasn't the cure I hoped for, I was afraid that I wouldn't think clearly enough to do anything. So I went to see an alternative medicine provider, a functional medicine person, and also a psychiatric nurse practitioner. Both of them have helped. You can see here [she points to an upper shelf] all the things I take to make my brain function. Altogether they cost me about $250 a month, with none of them covered by my insurance. I know now that I don't function well without them.

Barb: Are those things supplements?

Carol: They're a combination of supplements, amino acids, and herbs. They help me sleep more and have a more regular schedule. Because I have an ADD brain, I set an alarm for 3:00 pm, to remind me to take the pills so I can function for the afternoon and evening. All of these things have helped a lot.

Barb: It sounds as if they help you to structure your time and make decisions.

Carol: Yes. Making decisions can be hard for me. I wanted to experiment with my art, but I also wanted to do it with better materials. So I got inks, water colors, acrylics, different kinds of papers, and mat boards. I always carry me a little sketch book and ink pen, so I can draw anytime. I've been doing this for years. I continue to do the art while I'm waiting to get some of the equipment for the art studio.

Barb: Do you still have migraines?

Carol: Once or twice a week. I have trouble going to bed at night, if I forget to take these supplements. Sometimes I get a second wind at 11:00 pm, and before I know it, it can be 3:00 or 4:00 in the morning. When I'm into a piece of art work, hours pass before I know what time it is.

It can be frustrating to try to get things finished. It took more than a month between deciding to put this shelf up on the wall and actually finishing it. [She chuckles.] I also had a little bit of stress about you coming here to interview me, but I decided it would be okay. I moved some things around in the two days before you came!

Barb: I can relate to what you mention about getting things finished. I often leave things on my dining table for weeks. Then I invite friends over for dinner, so I will clean up and get all the papers off the table. For some of us who are creative types, we're not wired to do our best work at particular hours or in cubicles.

ALTERNATIVES TO SUICIDE GROUPS

As you know, we met at a meeting of the Alternatives to Suicide Peer Support group. I'd never heard of those before. How did you learn about them?

Carol: They had an open forum about altered states and suicide. At the forum the speaker was Susan Blauner, who had written the book *How I Stayed Alive When My Brain Was Trying to Kill Me.*[27] She talked about safety issues, including what is important to people, so they can feel comfortable talking about suicide. When I left the Suicide and Altered States forum I thought, "I don't have to hide anymore. I'm not alone."

The Recovery Learning Community started the Alternatives to Suicide peer support groups shortly after the forum.[28] It was my lifesaver; it gave me a place to be. My pattern had been to feel isolated and alone. I knew that isolation would kill me, if I didn't find a way to connect.

After being in Peer Support for six months or so, I felt ready to do more. For me, this was the perfect time to come into the Massachusetts Coalition for the Prevention of Suicide. I joined that movement and became active. I've gone to state conferences, been part of the local chapter, and worked at the Walkathon in support of people who have lost someone to suicide. All of these experiences have brought me to a clear decision. Whatever my brain is telling me, I will not allow my sons to become orphans because of suicide. I now have the tools and skills to work with those negative thoughts and keep them from taking over.

Barb: Good for you, Carol. You are an amazing woman! Thank you for sharing your story with me.

OTHER STORIES

———————◆———————

THROUGHOUT THIS BOOK, I have described a tsunami of the mind in terms of the killer waves of suicidal depression. In my own case, and those of the ten friends you have met here, the inner tsunamis can come as a shock, much like the oceanic tsunamis that follow undersea earthquakes. Three other stories from different times and places help to expand the picture of these human experiences. **Trauma.** Beloved comedian and actor Robin Williams ended his life in August 2014, soon after learning that he had early-stage Parkinson's disease**. Recovery.** In the biblical accounts of Jesus and the Gerasene demoniac, the story reveals the process of a person in crisis becoming able to return to community. **Hope.** Young Aliesha's words about her experience, her resiliency, and her wisdom are a vivid example of someone in recovery offering encouragement to others who are struggling.

———◆———

Robin Williams
When Robin Williams died by suicide on August 11, 2014, millions of people were shocked. Our beloved comedian and actor had made us laugh for decades, ever since he arrived in 1978 as Mork on the television show "Mork and Mindy." Appropriately, Katie Couric introduced Robin at a 2002 benefit as "one of the funniest people on the planet - we're just not sure which planet."

This phenomenally gifted man's funny roles ranged from Popeye to Mrs. Doubtfire, from Patch Adams to Theodore Roosevelt. In his serious roles, including the Oscar-winning psychiatrist in "Good Will Hunting" and his last film, "Boulevard," his emotional range was as impeccable as his timing.

Like many comedians, this man had more sides than his audience knew. He reported more than once that he had gone into treatment for alcohol and drug abuse. Family and friends also knew of his times of depression, and he had heart valve replacement surgery a number of years before his death. Importantly, Robin was also known for his empathy and dedication to helping others, as shown in his many visits to active-duty military and to severely ill children in hospitals.

After Robin Williams' suicide, various writers commented on what might have been happening inside this beloved performer's brain. His many performances fit some of the features of a bipolar illness, such as his manic energy and his ability to make up new ideas constantly. His reported struggles with alcohol and other drugs are not unusual for someone with a mood disorder. Many people develop substance issues as they try to calm their racing minds or get relief from their depression. Co-occurring disorders (substance abuse plus another illness such as depression) are now talked about more widely, but not all drug and alcohol treatment centers address the complex internal brain activity that lies behind a person's substance issues.

Evidence suggests that more people have bipolar depression or Bipolar Two than manic depression or Bipolar One. But media reports and casual conversation still imply that "bipolar" equals violent or delusional. With more stigma attached to the term "mental illness" than to substance abuse, Robin Williams may have chosen to talk about - or even to pursue - the more accepted kind of treatment.

Not long before his suicide, Robin received a diagnosis of early-stage Parkinson's disease. For a man famous for his quick speech, fast movements, and perfect timing, that diagnosis must have been traumatic for him. Parkinson's disease damages the area of the brain controlling movement and coordination, as well as speech. Given that dire prognosis, could Robin have reached a point where he could not imagine himself being disabled in the very ways he had excelled and delighted the world? After his death, an autopsy revealed that he had Lewy Body Dementia, a condition similar to Parkinson's disease.[29]

Many Americans hesitate to talk about brain illnesses, and especially suicide. We will never know for sure what was in Robin Williams' mind at the time of his death. But what we can do, remembering his talent and imagining his pain, is to learn more about the complexity of human brains,[30] and to work together to help others heal and survive.

———

Jesus and the Man with Demons

The Bible has over two hundred references to "unclean spirits," and the New Testament refers frequently to demons. One widely known reference is to Mary Magdalene, from whom seven demons had gone out. A less familiar healing story in three of the New Testament Gospels uses the term "demoniac" to describe a man who has a life-changing encounter with Jesus.

The three gospel accounts, Mark 5:1-20, Matthew 8:28-34, and Luke 8: 26-39, refer to Jesus' meeting someone suffering with demons, a man who has been living in the tombs. Jesus casts out the demons and sends them into swine, and the swine run into the sea and drown. In Matthew's version two men come out of the tombs. In Mark and Luke, one man comes to meet Jesus as Jesus steps off the boat into Gentile territory.

We can only guess what led the Gerasene man into the tombs. Mark says no one could restrain him any longer, even with a chain. He was howling and bruising himself with stones. In all three versions of the story, the man sees Jesus and bows down before him. Jesus asks his name, and in both Mark and Luke the man says his name is Legion, "for we are many." Luke describes the man as a person from the city who has had demons for a long time. "For many times it had seized him; he was kept under guard and bound with chains and shackles, but he would break the bonds and be driven by the demon into the wilds." (Luke 8:29, New Revised Standard Version).

The behavior of the man in this story may be an early account of a brain disorder. It might suggest someone with paranoid schizophrenia, since he is naked, shouting, strong enough to break his restraints, and living in the tombs. Today such a person could be in jail, prison, a state hospital, or hiding out in the woods.

The details in this situation are disturbingly familiar. Restraint and seclusion are still used on troubled people, despite evidence that these actions worsen the effects of trauma.

In all three gospel accounts the swine tenders run off to the village to tell what they have seen with Jesus and the drowned pigs. In Matthew's version the whole town comes out to meet Jesus, begging him to leave their neighborhood. But Mark and Luke say something different. When the villagers come to see what has happened, "they found the man from whom the demons had gone sitting at the feet of Jesus, clothed and in his right mind" (Luke 8:35, NRSV).

How did this amazing recovery happen? We aren't given many details. We can understand that the villagers might have been fearful about this mysterious event and this unknown healer. Could the man they know as a demoniac now be "normal?" And who is this alien miracle-worker? While the villagers show a mixture of curiosity and fear, the man himself is grateful. He asks to continue to be with Jesus. But Jesus says no. He wants the man to return to his village and tell what God has done for him.

From a biblical perspective, having the man tell his story in Gentile territory symbolizes the Christian gospel being spread beyond the borders of Jewish territory. But in the context of this book, that story goes farther. It shows that a spiritual connection with others is essential for healing and recovery after trauma. Jesus is present with the man, listens to him, and after the demons are removed, Jesus stays around long enough to encourage the man to return to his community. The villagers' resistance also reflects the fact that change is not always easy for other people to understand. But the demoniac is more than his illness. The story highlights how recovery is a process that involves a community, and is not a one-time event.

In Aleisha's Words

"I was a terrible two year old, awkward adolescent, defiant teenager. I am a daughter, a grandbaby, a sister, an employee. The library is my church, and running is my meditation. I'm very healthy, young, and normal. What comes to mind when you think of somebody living with a mental illness? Take a closer look.

I'm starting to learn the difference between myself and the werewolf I've been running from and turning into. Madness can weave itself in among my days, sometimes loud and other times hidden. This transformation of the mind is a fog bank that rolls in like the weather. It's frightening, disappointing, and often embarrassing. It's not a problem of morals or sin or salvation. It's a medical issue with a biological base. I call it the werewolf in the room. Sometimes I think I should just rent a room with iron bars on the windows during the full moon!

Two years ago I decided to kill myself. I was self-medicating and slipped out of touch. My decisions were coming from me, but I wasn't there. My first suicide attempt was within one year of starting treatment. My third attempt was a month after seeing my doctor. A sick mind doesn't always want help, and sometimes a person doesn't know how to ask for it.

Sometimes you can't prevent suicide, but don't be afraid and don't stop trying. Start with empathy. Look at and listen to the person, and do your best at being a non-judging, accepting, intuitive human being instead of searching for a specific illness label. People like me don't always show signs and symptoms of being close to suicide. Suicidal ideation and behavior is like the flu. It doesn't mean that the person will be sick forever, but it's a real illness that takes over the whole person.

If you're like me, you may have gone to your general practitioner asking for help with something you've tried to hide or deny for years. If you complain of symptoms, your doctor may try to treat each symptom. A specialist would know to treat the causative brain activity with an appropriate mood stabilizer. We can't expect people not specializing in dealing with these complicated brain-related issues to fix our problem right away.

Finding a provider and helpful ways to manage your struggles is easier if you can reach out to people who live in the community and have experienced these conditions. Amazing help is out there, but you have to play an active role in your recovery. I know now that if I don't take responsibility to do what I can to keep healthy, chances are high that I'll slip into a dark turn of mind. So I need to make sure I surround myself with people who care, letting them know what can happen to me so they can pick up the slack when I'm unable. That's not easy, because so much of what happens in brain-based disorders is still a mystery to most of us.

People generally do not understand the reality of brain-based disorders, due to conventional language and limited education about the mind. But there's good news as well. This is a revolutionary time in the study of the brain. New and more effective treatments are being discovered, and entire schools of thought are being rearranged. I'm more positive about treatment after a number of less effective efforts. If you or someone you know is thinking about seeking treatment, I encourage you to do so. If at first it doesn't seem like a fit, look for a better doctor. They are out there!"

NOTES

1. Parker Palmer, *Let Your Life Speak: Listening for the Voice of Vocation* (San Francisco: Jossey-Bass, 2000), 58.

2. American Psychiatric Association, *Diagnostic and Statistical Manual of Mental Disorders*, 5th Edition (Washington, DC: American Psychiatric Publishing, 2013).

3. Daniel Siegel, MD. *Mindsight: The New Science of Personal Transformation* (New York: Bantam, 2010).

4. Antonio Damasio, PhD, *The Feeling of What Happens: Body and Emotion in the Making of Consciousness* (New York: Harcourt Brace, 1999).

5. Jill Bolte Taylor, *My Stroke of Insight* (New York: Penguin, 2008).

6. The National Alliance on Mental Illness, www.nami.org.

7. Rose Rosetree, *Empowered by Empathy: 25 Ways to Fly in Spirit* (Sterling VA: Women's Intuition Worldwide, 2001).

8. NAMI FaithNet is an information exchange network focused on creating welcoming faith communities. See www.nami.org/faithnet.

9. Thomas Insel, MD, "Special Session," NAMI National Convention, Seattle WA, June 27, 2012.

10. Dr. Helen Mayberg reported on the microsurgeries on Charlie Rose's Brain Series 2, #7, "Depression," May 29, 2012, on Public Broadcasting System stations.

11. Kay Redfield Jamison, *Touched with Fire: Manic-Depressive Illness and the Artistic Temperament* (New York: Free Press, 1993).

12. Robin Williams' death occurred August 11, 2014, and was reported on major television and radio networks within 24 hours.

13. Empowerment and Peer Support are components of the Consensus Statement on Mental Health Recovery from SAMHSA, Substance Abuse and Mental Health Services Administration.

14. Ronald Fieve, MD, *Bipolar Breakthrough;* revised edition of *Bipolar II* (New York: Rodale, 2009).

15. Photograph courtesy of Rainy Day Images.

16. Philip Zimbardo et al, *The Time Cure: Overcoming PTSD with the New Psychology of Time Perspective* (San Francisco: Jossey-Bass, 2012).

17. Insel, "Special Session."

18. See *The Heart & Soul of Change: What Works in Therapy, 2d ed.* (Washington, DC: American Psychological Association, 2010).

19. Fieve, *Bipolar Breakthrough* was originally titled *Bipolar II*.

20. DBSA, the Depression and Bipolar Support Alliance, is online at www.dbsalliance.org

21. Questionnaire results reported to the author in 2014. Research also suggests that mirror neurons in the brain are the root of empathy. Siegel, *Mindsight,* pp. 59-63.

22. Al-Anon Family Groups are found online at www.alanon.org.

23. Alateen groups can be found at www.alateen.org

24. Webinars can be found online at the Suicide Prevention Resource Center, SPRC, which is part of SAMHSA, the national Substance Abuse and Mental Health Services Administration. The website is www.moodtracker.com

25. Mood Tracker website is www.moodtracker.com

26. Emotions Anonymous website is www.emotionsanonymous.org

27. Susan Rose Blauner, *How I Stayed Alive When My Brain Was Trying to Kill Me* (New York: William Morrow, 2001).

28. The Recovery Learning Community of Western Massachusetts developed the Alternatives to Suicide Peer Support Groups, held in four communities including Greenfield, MA.

29. "Robin Williams: Inside His Hidden Life," by Louise Barile (Closer Magazine, June 13, 2016)

30. New brain research has identified the habenula, a tiny place in the cerebellum, as being active when a person has both depression and suicidal thoughts.

BOOKS

Angst: Origins of Anxiety and Depression. Jeffrey P. Kahn, MD. Oxford, 2013.

The Biology of Desire: Why Addiction Is Not a Disease. Marc Lewis, PhD. Public Affairs, 2015

Bipolar Breakthrough. Ronald R. Fieve, MD. Rodale, 2009. Originally *Bipolar II.* Rodale, 2006.

The Body Keeps the Score: Brain, Mind, and Body in the Healing of Trauma. Bessem van der Kolk, MD. Penguin Books, 2014.

Daring Greatly: How the Courage to Be Vulnerable Transforms the Way We Live, Love, Parent, and Lead. Brene Bown, PhD, LMSW. Gotham Books, 2012.

The Feeling of What Happens: Body and Emotion in the Making of Consciousness. Antonio Damasio, MD. Harcourt Brace, 1999.

How I Stayed Alive When My Brain Was Trying to Kill Me. Susan Rose Blauner. William Morrow, 2001.

In An Unspoken Voice: How the Body Releases Trauma and Restores Goodness. Peter A. Levine, PhD. North Atlantic, 2010.

Mindsight: The New Science of Personal Transformation. Daniel J. Siegel, MD. Bantam, 2010.

My Stroke of Insight: A Brain Scientist's Personal Journey. Jill Bolte Taylor, PhD. Penguin Books, 2008.

Out of the Nightmare: Recovery from Depression and Suicidal Pain. David L. Conroy, PhD. Authors Choice, 1991, 2006.

Proust Was a Neuroscientist. Jonah Lehrer. Boston: Houghton Mifflin, 2007.

Radical Acceptance: Embracing Your Life with the Heart of a Buddha. Tara Brach, PhD. Bantam Books, 2003.

Upside: The New Science of Post-Traumatic Growth. Jim Rendon. Touchstone, 2015.

WEBSITES

www.afsp.org   American Foundation for Suicide Prevention.

www.myasha.org   ASHA International; Gayathri Ramprasad.

www.bipolarhappens.com   Julie A. Fast

www.bphope.com   Website for BP Quarterly Magazine.

www.bringchange2mind.com   Glenn Close.

www.cartercenter.org   Rosalyn Carter.

www.copelandcenter.com   Mary Ellen Copeland

www.dbsa.org   Depression and Bipolar Support Alliance

www.esperanza.com   Website for *Esperanza* Quarterly Magazine

www.ffront@uw.edu   Forefront: Innovations in Suicide Prevention

www.healthyplace.com   A Healthy Place

www.mha.org   Mental Health America

www.mentalhealthfirstaid.org

www.mentalhealthministries.net   Rev. Susan Gregg-Schroeder.

www.nami.org   National Alliance on Mental Illness

www.samhsa.gov/recovery/   Substance Abuse & Mental Health Services Administration

www.sprc.org   Suicide Prevention Resource Center.

www.twloha.com   To Write Love on Her Arms

www.tac.org   Treatment Advocacy Center

www.tic.org   Trauma Informed Care Project

www.wrap.org   Wellness Recovery Action Program

www.yspp.org   Youth Suicide Prevention Program. Seattle WA.

———

Crisis Text Line Go To 741-741

National Suicide Prevention Hotline   1-800-273-8255 (TALK)

www.crisischat.org

ACKNOWLEDGMENTS

I HAVE ALWAYS loved stories. I started by reading Nancy Drew mysteries as a child. Many years later, I switched from studying English literature at Yale to listening to the stories of senior citizens, college students, and spiritual leaders wanting to speak effectively from the pulpit. Listening carefully is my passion. That is one reason I prefer accompanying others rather than playing piano solos. *Tsunami of the Mind* has evolved over nearly a decade of hearing other people's stories and sharing my own story with many of them. I'm grateful for all of these conversations. I also value Dave Isay's *Story Corps* books as one model for conversations between regular people as they talk about their lives.

I WANT TO acknowledge the importance of three people who kept me moving on this project when I was too fearful or too disorganized to bring it to print. My daughter Joanna Nadeau and my friend DJ Bogue read sections and listened with care, often finding words that made more sense than my own. Local author Kevin Heimbigner also offered an expert's eye at a key time. Their support is beyond measure.

Finally, I choose to acknowledge by name a number of people who are not available to read this book. I celebrate their lives and regret their passing. Each of them was gifted and loved, but I believe their pain was too great at a particular moment for them to imagine staying alive. Among the many people we have lost to suicide, I want to remember Matt Adler, Winona Helen-Lehua Ani, Jennifer Bergeson, Julie Brown, Travis Christman, Andrew Crichton, Terry Elliott, Pat McAfee, Sara Morley, Kathy Rook, Jim Siebold, and Brandon Soule. They are a reminder to all of us that love is never wasted.

ABOUT THE AUTHOR

BARBARA BATE IS a gifted teacher, writer, musician, and spiritual guide. She studied at the College of Wooster, Yale University, the University of Oregon, and McCormick Seminary. She has won awards for her public speaking, college teaching, and preaching. She founded the Women's Studies Program at Northern Illinois University in 1980, as an assistant professor of speech communication. She also taught at Yale University, the University of Oregon, Princeton Seminary, Drew University, and United Theological School in Harare, Zimbabwe.

Her many publications include *Communication and the Sexes*, Harper Collins, 1988, 2d. ed. Waveland, 1997; *Women Communicating*, Ablex,

1988; *Freedom in the Pulpit, Discipleship Resources, 1996;* and the video series *Leading in the Spirit,* Discipleship Resources, 1997. She lives in Ocean Park, Washington. She has been the board president for Willapa Counseling Center, NAMI Pacific County, and NAMI Washington. She is a certified facilitator for Wellness Recovery Action Plan (WRAP) and NAMI Connection Recovery Support Groups. She is also a piano accompanist for community musicals, choral groups, and vocal and instrumental soloists. Her daughter and son-in-law live in upstate New York.